AN ASSIGNATION
WIT DY TRUTH

selected poems and stories

1964 – 2007

by
JACOB BUSH

meta one

A CIP record for this book is available from
the British Cataloguing in Publication Data Office.

ISBN 978-0-9556060-0-7

Printed on acid-free archive quality paper
and bound by ProPrint, Carmarthen.

for Miryam
who reminded me
how to look at stars

Photograph by fellow poet Lael Silbert
Published in Sanskaras

CONTENTS

STORIES

with friends in st. ives

" 'if you cannot bring
good news, then
don't bring any.' "
                    - Bob Dylan

"Still, you know words
ought to mean more
than we express when
we use them, so a
whole book ought to
mean a great deal
more than the writer
meant"
                    - Lewis Carroll

"And so I always bear the cup
If, haply, mine may be the drop -
Some pilgrim thirst to slake -"
                    - Emily Dickinson

I was born under an alias in Brooklyn, New York in 1928.

After knocking around various undergraduate and postgrad facilities (majoring in chemistry, literature, mathematics and psychology) and working at jobs ranging from farm hand, factory worker and warehouseman to statistician, I emigrated to a variety of countries, finally settling in western Wales.

I've read my work from public platforms in the United States, Britain, continental Europe and on the high seas. Any number of early poems were broadcast on radio station WNYC. Several of the poems and short stories in this collection have appeared in New Poetry 3 (Arts Council of Great Britain), Planet (The Welsh Internationalist), Sanskaras, Hyn Poetry Quarterly, Gyro World Scope Quarterly, Hyn Anthology, Cabaret 246, Merlin, Touch and Go, Home Planet News, Education Otherwise publications, Loose Change and Roundyhouse.

THE SOLOMON OF THE GUTTER won the S.E. Wales Writers Umbrella Short Story Competition and was subsequently published in Planet, as were THE FEAR OF RAPE and some of my poems. "1918" and "hill resident, global village" won the top prizes in the 1998 W. Wales Poetry Competition, subsequently appearing in Merlin.

Poems and stories should be viewed in historical context. Spellings, except for deliberate "errors" and the odd one which may have escaped my scrupulous proofreading, are largely American whenever American and British spellings are different.

Thanks are due to old friends from Cabaret 246, the Welsh Union of Writers, et cetera, to older friends from the New York Poets Co-operative and the Poets of Gansevoort Pier and others too numerous to mention.

A series of illnesses and resultant disabilities delayed completion of this collection in its present form while providing a kind of counterpoint for some of the earlier work. It eventually became self-evident that I needed help from an expert, so I called in my long-time friend and associate, John Bilsborough, a fine poet, publisher, visual artist, historian and event-maker, to help me get some of my house in order. The result is Meta, a sporadic magathology, of which this is issue number one.

Noreen was an Irish American barmaid in Barcelona who became a research assistant at the New York advertising agency I worked at. She died in a car crash. Her epitaph is a villanelle except that, the tercets being haiku, the terminal quatrain is permitted to flower into a tanka.

There are a few works of merit that should be in this book but that I can't find just now. More than forty years is long enough to wait. Hopefully they will appear along with other authors in some future issue of Meta.

Jacob Bush, Pontyates, Carmarthenshire. 2007

fragment

and what do you mean by real
and any ancient child will tell you
rapunzel lies in wait, her hair
will pierce today the sacred floor

<u>prologue</u>

she laughed a golden apricot
and a hundred giraffes of turquoise dreams
unleashing unicorns on plastic avenues
drenched in a sun where even robber kings
once viewed intricacies and saw extravaganzas
in the eyes of solid stone springbok
and the machine of time kept punching holes
into non-existent paper but
she laughed a golden apricot

bop for a bushy bush

the hitchhiking coyote was a stationary gypsy

for the auto moved as the coyote stood still

relative to the auto which moved

relative to the surface

of the earth which moved relative to the sun

which moved relative to vega

who never heard of the coyote

whose ordered life was disorganised

as mine

my life

bombed out by memoranda

and layoff slips

and time sheets

and unemployment books

and nervous typewriters

and wretched moods of bread and dread

and exultant moods of death

and ecstatic moods of life

and my bureau drawers are bursting with fishbones

and coyote parking tickets

<u>nuclear psychoneurosis</u>

1)
the world has been cruel to my mind
 has ravished my ecstasies with thunderbolts
shiva has lacerated the tendons of my brain
 & brings me a basket of bombs for breakfast
1000 automobiles collide with 1000 frank o'haras
in atman i carry the guilt of being god
i am job
i only followed orders
i have done nothing
 nothing at all
i fall to my knees
 & beg my own forgiveness

2)
i didn't mean to pick those flowers
i only meant to cheer over the death
 of babies in nagasaki
 to celebrate hiroshima
i was a teenage fascist
at 8 i dreamed of being dictator of the universe
 & castrated my father with a kitchen knife
 as we choked each other with words
i helped expel three blind saints from the
communist party
i seized the telegraph office
 only to pursue myself down endless corridors
gotta hang up now
see ya round the guillotine

3)
SIR
3 moons please
i need them for a stranger
    who lost the only moon she had
        (that's what she gets
        for trusting an astronaut)

how much?
    my soul you say?
here, take it
  .

  .

  .
there's plenty more where it came from

4)
i am a crowd
i impinge upon myself
    in disastrous isolation
i am a creature named traffic
    swirling in memories of cream
i traffic in second-hand harps
they don't make harps the way they used to
    (they never did)
    - - - hey, why don't we get stoned
      & wait for yesterday
tomorrow is frigid
)she never comes(

5)
i have been ambushed by a muse
she insists i skip lunch
    and write my poetry instead
i obey her by writing on the surface of the lake
with a swab of absorbent cotton ....
tonight i'll eat the shadow of the promise tree
tonight i'll confide in apricots

tomorrow morning the sun will go mad
    waiting for me to rise
        as i sleep till early last week

6)
i wonder how long i've been dead now
    (it's been several hours since my shoes stopped
hurting)
no, i haven't got a ticket
my passport is no longer valid
panting palaeozoic pythons
    populate my transelectric reveries
nothing matters but our elegance and tears
kiss me ... i'll go it again

7)
the psychoanalyst cooks a stew of clocks
    waiting for my return
he ladles out an alarm clock
    and some lightly buttered checks
witch doctors with poisoned spears
    read new yorkers in the waiting room
don't wait up for me
    i'll be back at the dawn of time

8)
there's no way to end eternity
      & that's that
did you know
      that exactly three infinite sets
      of concentric circles with irrational radii
      will cover an infinite plane
discus the implications for hyperspheres in 20 words
or less –
      mail in to god with 20 crackerjokes
      ---- pandora will open the prize ....

9)
the world has been cruel to my mind
      has ravished my ecstasies with thunderbolts
shiva has lacerated the tendons of my brain
      & brings me a basket of bombs for breakfast
1000 automobiles collide with 1000 frank o'haras
in atman i carry the guilt of being god
i am job
i only followed orders
i have done nothing
      nothing at all
i fall to my knees
      & beg my own forgiveness

maria

animals are only people who talk a different language
she said
writing the first line of my poem
(though she didn't have too much english)
& it never snows in buenos aires
though it's cold & wet in july ...
it's healthier
she said
to get your fingers done every month
instead of wait a year
& let your cuticles get coarse & jagged ...
she brushed her straight red hair from her face & smiled
attacking my thumb with pumice stone ...
you write
don't you
she said
then called over her little boy ...
look at the man
he's a writer
look at his funny shirt
she said
smile at him
say hello to him
maybe he'll write about you ....
or me

embarkation

and when i've made it to the mountain
will i hide
in a cave
in its side
or will
i place my flag upon the mountaintop

shall i be a holy man
silently peeling potatoes
or shall i buy a canvas & some oils
and imitate the sun

how many clouds
can dance on the head of one ego

shall i discard my voice
having become the all
freed from the need for communication
or shall i prove to the blackbirds that i can sing

does the ocean care
have the clouds held a plebiscite
what is the opinion
of the mountain

<u>devotional in blue</u>

how shall i count the lion eggs
number the elephant blossoms
to put in my weary chariot
for my hands are blistered by fires
of unnecessary evils
and my mind is weighed down by dreams
and my dreams are buried by ballots
and they shall cut off my head to free me
from non-existent leisure
and i think a lot about the universe
but it never thinks about me
and i dream that i am a motorboat
a bolt of cloth or a bicycle
riding without a rider
or the sunlight on your plate
and i ride against flannel knights
laying waste their candy-coated world
yet feeding dreams to my typewriter
hallucinations to my pen
and put my paranoia in a purple vase
but how shall i count the lion eggs
or comb my copper and cobalt soul

the journey

i've stumbled onto some secrets
& then forgotten them
since the discovery of an occult fact
abolishes it

there is only one fact ...
i found it near the gutter one day
i hung it up in the sun
i painted it royal blue

sparrows bring telegrams
anger is indispensable
i am the sound of one hand clapping
i beat the sun with roses

i work feverish ... my purpose convoluted
i am a turtle
my suitcase was empty when i started out
and now it's filled with stars

if i knew
and if i told you
where the grail was hidden
how then would you spend your life

<u>search for a solution</u>
<u>of the firing squad synchronisation problem</u>

(excerpts from a book description,
united states department of commerce
clearinghouse announcements
in science and technology
#29. operations research ...
A FOUND POEM)

to solve the conceptually difficult

firing squad synchronisation problem

each of the four attempts has in common

a clerical checking program

and a basic backtrack program

for searching the solution space ...

serial definition ...

entirely computer-directed

functional planning

and constraint satisfaction ...

man-machine symbiotic ...

to control

and direct ...

the computer search

rhyme

shall we build the tower of babel
we'll build it out of ego stones
opaque glass and sinister plastic
neanderthal tusks & dinosaur bones
old jet engines ... dissertations
novels ... songs ... & several poems
40,000,000 generations
leaving their ancestral homes
40,000,000 princely princes
transterrestrial sonar rabble
bearing bricks in dayglo coffins
to construct the tower of babel

shall we build the tower of babel
we'll build it out of rocket ships
magic rubies burning sapphires
transcelestial acid trips
substochastic meditations
silkworms living in transistors
avatars from distant planets
come to life as draft resisters
avatars from distant planets
playing transmolecular scrabble
weaving sunbeams into windows
to construct the tower of babel

shall we build the tower of babel
we'll build it out of garbage cans
crystals shining bright each morning
memoranda ... secret plans
kabalistic manifestations
neognostic rock & roll
transgalactic federations
in the cloakroom of the soul

transgalactic federations
never known to merely dabble
mining mysteries on saturn
to construct the tower of babel

shall we build the tower of babel
we'll build it out of birds & trees
subways without destinations
pretty girls with sexy knees
ploughshares beat into computers
kettles having learned to dream
princesses with many suitors
robots who have learned to scream
princesses with many suitors
flying throwrugs meant for travel
sanding several complex numbers
to construct the tower of babel

shall we build the tower of babel
we'll build it out of goodly tents
condominiums on the marshes
charging transcerebral rents
poets reading to each other
in a subterranean room
krishna singing to his mother
of the world's impending doom
krishna singing to his mother
bearing secrets to unravel
swimming to the ocean bottom
to construct the tower of babel

radio noah

i am a phosphorescent tree
i am a metaphysical flashlight battery
i echo moonlight
i have been green leaves in the suntime
i am the song
the nest
the robin
my chest is the sun itself
i dine on worms ...
i am a cancer cell
a revolution
a symphony
a rock cantata in a mafia bar and grill
i am a sainted madman
i am a faustus drunk on kabala
i am gnostic & coptic
i was immaculately conceived in the womb of marx
i am both mohammed and mountain
i am a man and a woman caressing each other
in sulphured smog
i am a serpent in eden and my name is man
i am brilliant blazing apricots & the epistemology of pebbles
i am cohesion and adhesion
consciousness & perception in a burnt out matchstick
my name is ralph waldo emerson & i am vibrance in the mud

i am immanuel kant rapping with jung & freud
i am a conversation with your sicilian friend
i am the lust of all men for all women
i am a reflective ear
through my particularity
i am the all
i sing in the chorus of god ...
i am the poem behind the sine curve
the choreography of oscilloscopes
a troll whispering to mushrooms ...
i kneel in the chapel for i am spartacus
i am a marigold seeking forgiveness
perhaps i've been nostradamus
i am the sea that dashes inside your mind
i am ineffable sailing boats
i am a universal laser
localised to careening typewriter keys
geographied in –
the invisible wind

smiling decipede standing at ease '68

<u>on returning to my apartment on calle quevedo</u>
<u>after a visit to the american consulate</u>

a norse god tore out one eye
and into the blood dipped phoenix feathers
to burn for the time of year
and so remembering
i left the house of rules
and entering on its kingdom
i met oedipus on the road
but the norse god tore out
but one eye

i saw a boy today
and he carried a platter upon his head
all filled with things to eat
and he climbed a hill
and i tell you his feet had been twisted backward
slowly scream by scream in his infant days ...
buy from my boy. señor
buy from the crippled boy

my head has been twisted scream by scream
my name is wotan woden odin
i am hercules in the cave
      samson on the guillotine
      jonah regurgitated by the whale
i am a little boy

i walked on the soil of the country of my exile today
i took a twig ... i scratched VIETNAM-CAMBODIA-LAOS
into the ground...
oh land of napalm and untwisted feet :
there's no place like home

intercontinental ballistic daffodils

i've walked in caverns of the sea
pursued by my relentless mind
and neptune's daughter speaks to me
her voice is harsh and most unkind
and i have been to old pompeii
where voices of a fiery past
pour lava on a child at play
and drown his dreams in sudden blast
and there in a valley bright and green
i've trod on ants who wished to live
snuffed out by terrors scarcely seen
my mindless random footsteps give
and i have met an algerian lad
stranded on tunisian soil
who told me of the life he had
before his fortunes came to boil
and i have walked in valleys old
shadowed by the golden rif
and there i met some travelers bold
sitting in a cloud of kif

who told me of their sacred dreams

who told me of their fiery past

and i have seen the marble fist

and come from the land of iroquois

where man-made poisons fill the mist

where music bleeds in city noise

and i have been to napoli

and there they found me very weird

and little children laughed at me

and pointed to my shaggy beard

and i sell laughter to the sky

and tell my dreams to distant stars

and i'll tread water till i die

and meditate in noisy bars

and i'll fetch rubies from the fire

and flowers from the burning ash

and i shall risk the devil's ire

and drive the griffins from my path

and run beneath the restless sea

pursued by my relentless mind

where neptune's daughter speaks to me ...

her voice is harsh and most unkind

ganesha in a croatian graveyard

the cemetery is a place for life
and we five fires burn brightly on the hilltop
and ingrid christina is pregnant in the moonlight
and laughs with a bellyfull of life

sheepdogs converse with the clouds of the horizon
as we sit in the half-light of the three-quarter moon
and dream of electrifying the mausoleum
and making it a citadel-shrine of our lives

oh we shall feed our passions to the stars that singe
    the adriatic sky
and we shall slice our bread and cheese on tombstones
and let our vermouth bottle sound as a ram's horn in the night
and let our elegant turkish pipe of lebanese hashish
    serenade the dead

tape recorder batteries awaken in the impending dew
conjuring janis joplin and indian sitars above the maze
    of medieval streets
as red and blue are implicit in every grey ... and we sway
in the international dawn

<u>thoughts during a dalmatian hurricane</u>

PAPRIKASH PAPRIKASH
     the paprikash lady smiles her warmth
     into the balkan hurricane
     a simple lady this
     a simple life ...
     who is to say
     that she's not more important
     than tolstoi

ZHIVINA ZHIVINA
     the poultry man
     glares at the wind

what is a sailor
     a sailor is the sea ...
     he conquers the wind
     by becoming it

how do you expect me
     to neatly stack my thoughts
     in a hurricane ...
     i tried it once
     and they toppled over

distant india is sculpted of this wind
     and you'd better believe it
     you there with your eyes full of atman
     and you with your technological snide

i am bitter in the wind
       i am only a writer
       i am not even tolstoi
       so, even more than tolstoi
       i am less than the paprikash lady

the truth of the matter
       is that i know nothing ...
       i am informed of this
       by the noisy clatter of things
       in the chaotic wind

i am an existential grasshopper
       with broken feet ...
       kirkegaard is dead
       and all my idols are crumbling

the sun will shine through my door
       for my door will blow away

PAPRIKASH PAPRIKASH
       the paprikash angel smiles her warmth
       into the balkan hurricane
       a simple lady this
       a simple life ...
       who is to say that the fire of her smile
       cannot conquer the wind

<u>and the whirlpool drives the prayerwheel</u>

(title by dylan thomas)

what am i but a pair of wings

what am i but a creature who bursts

out of velvet dungeons

breaking chains made of rainbows

what am i but a pair of wings

that tear relentlessly into lunatic skies

icarus often despondent

prometheus often filled with joy

what am i but a pair of wings

a nightflyer in hurricanes

a navigator without maps

intoxicated on amorphous destinations

what am i but a pair of wings

electing goals less relevant than the unknown road

rejoicing the dampest intimations of spring

throwing open my coat to the still chill air of dying winter

what am i but a pair of wings

and what does it matter whether i get

where i dream that i'm going

when the point is that i can fly

In zwei Jahren nach Amerika

favorittenstrasse funk

(favorittenstrasse was named by a
former austro-hungarian emperor)

favorittenstrasse,
the vienna no one mentions in the travel brochures ...
is it possible that it was ever
anybody's favorite ...
a long wide dismal street in the 10th district
neither suburb nor heart of town ...
impoverished furniture stores
grim grey buildings on the verge of weeping

i sit on the 167 tram & look out of the window
the ghost of william blake sits next to me
reciting "on another's sorrow" ...
the street is embarrassed
and hides its identity whenever possible
behind signs proclaiming names of imagined squares
as if ashamed to proclaim its own preposterous name

more diversity here among those who shun diversity
than one could find at a convention of individualists ...
that couple there with the baby carriage
trying to look brave ...
those yugoslav street workers who will never know
the name of hope or what it is
to own a bathtub ...
in drunken pain
smiling into the smog

these crumbling buildings
sighing into the watered sunshine
of a chilling spring

sutra in metered rhyme

rejoice, the sky's a lovely shade of grey
the rain that falls will cause a flower's birth
and human tears, though some will fall today
will surely bring some comfort to the earth

i think i'll paint today, although i'm blind
with pigments that i've salvaged from the mud
i've got a little canvas in my mind
i've got a brush i'll dip into my blood

i'll paint a dream of blue and red and gold
they're stored here in the warehouse of my brain
i'll write a symphony while growing old
i'll love a little, just to ease the pain

i'll build a city out of human groans
i'll cook a curry salted with my tears
the universe must love us through its moans
it wears a giant necklace made of years

the dolphins dance, though doomed they still must play
though every silver lining has its shroud
the sky above's a lovely shade of grey
we'll dance bright blue and do it very proud

rejoice, the sky's a lovely shade of grey
the rain that falls will cause a flower's birth
and human tears, though sure to fall today
will surely bring some comfort to the earth

the cathedral

oh, yes, the cathedral. not the scheming in corridors and
council rooms but the cathedral itself. not the tithes,
the taxes, the grants, the wages, the federal money.
not the exploitation of the peasantry to accumulate the
gold out of which to fashion elegant sensual handcuffs
for artists and their audiences but the very cathedral
and nothing else. not that case full of medals over there,
not the sceptre nor the ecclesiastical robes nor the hippie
costumes nor the suits and ties nor the tuxedos nor the
stained glass windows. not the torture rack in the basement,
the holy grail in the attic, the piece of the true cross,
the bark of the buddha tree, the staff of solomon, the knife
with which the wisest of men murdered an innocent infant,
not the aroma of burning saints - only the cathedral.
not the building nor the grounds nor the employees nor the
hierarchy nor the congregation nor the police nor even
entirely the anarchists plotting poetry in the toilet or
the children smoking acrid weeds around the spire - but
the cathedral, the cathedral, it's the cathedral i'm talking
about, not the bricks, not the stone, not the wind nor the
sky nor the sunshine nor the rain nor even the rainbow.
not the deaths, not the lives but the cathedral. not even
the father, the son, the holy ghost, the virgin mary, the
sacred hag or shiva. not the devil, the angel, the bag of
marbles, the complete set of war bubble gum cards, the order
of the british empire, but the cathedral. not the cathedral's
abstract qualities, not its history, neither recognition
nor money, comfort nor sanity, orgasms nor kaleidoscopes,
not the atomic bomb, not the population explosion, not love,
not friendship, not enemyship. nor hot nor cold nor starvation
nor halva nor magic mushrooms nor passover wine, nor tortures
nor ecstasies - not even the cathedral, yet only the cathedral,
it's just the cathedral i'm talking about.

pantoum forty-two

ask any painter about the smell of his turpentine

ask a poet who caresses his typewriter like a stradivari

ask a girl in love with a dandelion

ask your freaked out creator whether he's sorry

ask a poet who caresses his typewriter like a stradivari

ask st christopher whether he believes in god

ask your freaked out creator whether he's sorry

to have plucked you out of an electronic pod

ask st christopher whether he believes in god

ask st mary whether it was right

to have plucked you out of an electronic pod

to glitter like an ornament in the night

ask st mary whether it was right

ask a girl in love with a dandelion

to glitter like an ornament in the night

ask any painter about the smell of his turpentine

requiem for peggy frank

peggy frank is dead. she was a painter who bent colors in the intimated perspectives of happy rooms. she felt guilty sometimes about turning off the darkness when she'd enter her studio, when she'd pull the sunshine onto the canvas and make it sing. she drank a lot, she was an artist and artists don't have beautiful lives. she drank a lot at pubs with friends and she liked to talk and she liked to listen and she liked to think and, until the going got really tough, and she stopped drinking, she liked to complain. when every sale counted, she gave paintings to friends. She painted orange and blue and white and yellow and ...visions of our forgotten joys – chairs, tables, flowers, people, imploding canvasses, elliptical distortions, direct views, daytime, night, she was an artist and artists have beautiful lives – being less suited than other people to filling out forms, they have to fill out more of them. peggy frank was asked for descriptions of her paintings and sent them photos. i saw her living and i almost saw her die. i saw her near enough to the end that i could have told her secrets that i didn't dare to tell myself. instead she told me, lacking strength for words. she lived like the weather and died like a swan. she spoke to me. she spoke to you. she gave us parts of her soul. this whole world pulsates with her shapes and tones and colors ...this room ... every room ... peggy frank isn't dead.

dear mad beautiful renée's favorite nightmare

reality was renée's favorite nightmare and she loved it
with the joy of a mother. whenever she'd live in
reality, she could pick a rose, walk away and sniff it
without some sinister being jumping out from under a
rock and placing her under arrest - reality had laws a
shade more humane and so she adored it. reality was
renée's favorite nightmare and she loved it with the
joy of a lover. whenever she'd live in reality, she
could cross a bridge secure in the knowledge that it
was not an absolute certainty that it would blind her
with unnameable light she would call in her terror by
the buddha word of illumination. reality was just a bit
softer and she appreciated that. reality was renée's
favorite nightmare and she loved it with the joy of a
sister. she even got married, loved her husband,
kissed her radio, knew it wasn't watching her. hunger
never bothered her much. the great depression never
got her down. she knew the streets would only be on
fire if someone dropped a bomb or torched them.
torture was in exile and she never missed its poetry.
daffodils are as real as hobnailed boots and there is a
blessing in that. reality was renée's favorite
nightmare and she loved it with the joy of a daughter.
reality never ceased to amaze her in its improbability.
she hugged reality, kissed it deep and waltzed with it.
she rode on its shoulders like a little girl. renée loved
reality so much, she decided to stay with it for the rest
of her life. a strange decision, you might say - but
then what d'ya expect:
she was crazy!

another side of vincent van gogh

> "I have been in cities where
> the song was all I had, -"
> - edna st. vincent millay

there is one poet in the world, one composer, one painter, one sculptor, one whatever you call it. there is one artist in the world and we are all with our brushes, our chisels, our typewriters, our guitars, our other working tools, only his cosmic stenographers. some of us take dictation better than others, some of us hear it a little different but we are all (those of us not reduced by the office politics of the spirit) just secretaries, our so-called creations discoveries in the blinding light of ecstasy, groping revelations in the darkness of anguish, blurred visions in the half-light of life. we all explore the same themes and every man and woman of us has his joan, his arthur, his faustus, his christ, his buddha, his vincent van gogh. if you took every poem in which i've ever referred to or alluded to vincent van gogh and you laid them end to end or side by side and then you added every poem that any other poet has written about vincent and every song and every biography and every novel and every piece of art criticism and every painting that's been influenced by him, and every religious work and philosophical essay and psychodynamic treatise and every popular article and every personal letter and every movie still and every etcetera that in any way bore on vincent van gogh they would probably cover this planet several times over. yet he was no more than a man with a special way of seeing who did things with paint and canvas, ate paint, drank turpentine, courted sunstroke and prostitutes and god, lived in a city, cut off one of his ears, sought asylum in a small town in france, was persecuted by the locals. he was just some crazy stenographer doing his thing. exploring perennial themes to the point of death, he became a perennial himself. i forget which ear it was that vincent van gogh cut off though it hardly matters. artists are only people after all and people here and there in the world have always been encouraged to cut things off or cut things out: their hair, their tonsils, their ears, their eyes, their beards, their breasts, their foreskins, their appendices, their pineal glands, their frontal lobes, their clitori, their testicles, the cheeks of their asses, their fingernails and toenails, their hearts, their minds, their souls. they punch holes in themselves to hang ornaments or to fill with paint or drugs. people are people and they will never leave well enough alone. i live in a small town myself and the city comes to it and does so with much of its ferocity. i was awakened the other night by urban shrieks on the cobbled streets, by strange drunken cackles and weird aggressions, by the kind of screams that pursued vincent van gogh, entered him and killed him. under conditions like this you might ask why i don't live in the city itself. i lived in a city once and all my neighbours cut off both their ears.

in concert
WIZZ JONES
LAZY FARMER

JOHN JAMES

nigel jones
chrissie quayle
jake bush
st.ives
guildhall

8.00.
thursday july 31st

lemonmoon

lemonmoon
honeymoon in reverse gear
that quintessential moment
when each man & woman's an island
flashing moans in the night
tigers leaping forth from the mouths of former lovers
let's be friends, you bastard
let's be civilised, you bitch
look, she says, i'll let you keep more than half
          all the empty spaces are for you
listen, he says, and falls silent
i'll take that, she says, you wanted it
i'll give this, he says, you didn't ...
today, let's have breakfast together
all i want is a swallow of water & a gulp of air
which one of us is going to cook it
why didn't you ever tell me this before
why didn't you ever listen
you haven't changed
you've changed
i'll tell you what - we'll slice it down the middle
it's there
it's here
you call that love
          forcing a kiss on my neck where the vampire bites
have you ever
none of your business
i'm very tired
          it's been 17 years & i want some sleep

<u>endless river</u>

i must get back
i must get back
i must get back to the river
there are paradises to win
there are rainbows to sell
i have something
i have something
i have something to give her

it keeps flowing through me
i remember it well
though it's constantly constantly
constantly hidden
it's constantly constantly
constantly showing
it flows through my spirit
it flows through unbidden
and in deepest darkness
even then it is glowing

some call it ecstasy
some call it freedom
some call it semen
and some call it blood
it's a river that flows
through the unwritten story of
cascading moonbeams
and torrents of mud

on elegant mountains
in valleys of struggle
it justifies all
without justification
it's why blues are gorgeous
the reason for trouble
it's why we're fulfilled
in our deepest frustration

i have come here
i must stay here
i have returned to the river
though words are so fragile
i've something to tell
i've something
i've something
i've something to give her
this song that she taught me
i must sing it well

<u>why i had the biggest war bubble gum card collection in flatbush</u>

i know those guys. those guys who fought in the spanish civil
war. i knew those guys and i loved them and i hated them too.
so that's what you think. you think they went to spain because
they wanted to stop fascism. wanted to nip hitler in the bud.
prevent the second world war. that's what you think. when the
second world war came they didn't say "i told you so." they went
again. they died in salerno. they stormed anzio. they chased
desert foxes across africa. they never stopped. if they lived they
came home and they fought. and they fought. and they fought.
some ran guns for the hagana. some ran guns for the i.r.a. guns-
guns-guns-guns. they called them arms. loving arms. they
wanted to hold the world in their loving arms. they loved the
world and hated it with the love of an unrequited lover. they sent
each other to firing squads. expelled each other from the
communist party. called each other renegades and cut each other
down on the street. joined goon squads and fought scabs.
became professional anti-communists and joined private armies.
withdrew into corners and sulked and did the crossword puzzle.
what's a four letter word meaning interaction? kill.
no, what's a four letter word? maim. what's a four letter word?
kiss. fuck. love. they held the world in their fire arms. they
joined the lions and roared. they held machine guns with the
same defensive affection that they had with toy replicas when
they were little boys. bang-bang-bang-bang. they refused candy
and smoked cigars. imitated edward g. robinson imitating little
caesar imitating a guy who didn't care. imitated humphrey
bogart like i did when i was a teenager and wasn't old enough for
the war. cigarette dangling from lips. collar turned up.
i'm tough, see? i'm gene autry and i love my horse and i don't
need no kisses. i know those guys. they carry machine guns.
they're steel on the outside. soft as marshmallow on the inside.
made of rejected love.

you are wounded but not broken

let me read you your own verses that gave me the truth of your
viscera. let me sing your songs to you. let me remind you and
show you how to fly beneath the ground. come with me and we
shall find the warm and sunny places in this darkened universe.
injustice, yes, we shall not live with it - but against it or over and
under and around it - an old acquaintance, that. i have lived and
grown in spite of injustice for nearly half a century now in this
lifetime alone. before that, well, millennia of persecution of
blacks, irishmen, jews, arabs, lovers. injustice is the spur that
makes the horse of inner freedom gallop to the stars. arise o
pegasus and fly with me! something of this may be found in the
texture of existence itself. imbalances are brought into being for
the tedious frenzy of the quest for equilibrium. if equilibrium
were given at the start, there would be no me or you. consider the
oyster and the pearls he makes out of the ravishing inquisi-
tional irritation of countless grains of sand. if you and i were
oysters, we'd produce a galaxy of pearls together. these are
pearls - our insights, our poems. we are lamarckable giraffes
stretching our heads above the rising smog. do you know about
antiquing? furniture not quite weathered enough is beaten with
chains to make it rise in value. i loved you when you were a
bedside bureau and i was a chest of drawers. you never chose
this freedom march but were thrust into it when your mother
expelled you from her womb. she was lonely like god and
created another creature to love.
o, saint joan, don't let them burn you at the stake this time.
wear the protection of my love.

c'est la vie

that's the way the law operates, captain dreyfus.

we don't like you bloody alsatians, we only like

the minerals of your land. and though we're

addicted to pomp and ceremony, we prefer officers

who aren't jews like the gentle soldier

we nailed to the cross. we got our nails ready –

for your coffin – to ship you home at last from

devil's island, you devil you, ragged where you wished

to be immaculate, buttons torn from your chest

in disgrace. we had a reason to suspect your treason.

how could you possibly love us, who hated you?

you've paid your eighteen years so here is your medal

with a hypocritical kiss for each cheek.

that's the way the law operates, like the efficient killing

machine you joined to find release from silent death.

the law doesn't operate at all, captain dreyfus.

it maims.

the dandelion

legally, it's a weed, but i say it's a flower. its seed was taken as a symbol of freedom by whitman. the blossom itself is considered a nuisance around well-ordered english gardens, because of its chaotic nature, its unwillingness to stand in line like a member of the national service. the dandelion, random and anarchic, like the tall, unmowed grass itself, caressed by the wind. even the bloom is irregular, the countless jagged petals, golden like a sunburst and named for a lion's teeth. these soft dentures nip lovingly at the noonday breeze. the dandelion has been maligned for its color is as rich as that of the yellow tulip or of the golden daffodil, richer than that of the pale yellow rose and yet it is largely ignored or stigmatised by children of many countries with the culpability for their enuresis. i'm like the dandelion myself ... tried most of my life for the trimmed and regular garden of systematic philosophy; gave it up and found myself by growing wild. i sing no more of buddha or jesus but of the dandelion instead. miryam said the other day that there is yes in the spaces between the no's. well, in the field of yesses, the dandelion grows.

the lucky ones

they were the lucky ones. children together, they
came to each other without trial and error, without
hit or miss, without searching, without convoluted or
tedious accident, direct, spot on, out of a mutual
awakening, a perfect fit from the start. they were the
lucky ones. they were young parents when i met
them. it was their first house and his second job.
their two children had barely entered school.
their life was warm and green and tranquil and quiet.
they had their struggles like all young adults but they
were the lucky ones and they'd never known
anything but love. me, it was my second marriage,
my thirteenth home and i'd lost count of how many
jobs. i wasn't one of the lucky ones and rarely
seemed to get it right. i searched for affection in
impossible places and dug for love in the filthy
sawdust of the palace of eviscerated dreams. i told
him about it and he was jealous of the unknown
diamonds in my tears, curious of a world he'd never
known, eager to verify empirically and by means of
comparison the validity of a choice he'd never had to
make.
i warned him. told him i'd only spoken to him for
the comfort of unloading. i told him that the
phosphorous flares that illuminated the palace could
burn his flesh and mar his soul. but he was one of
the lucky ones and so he didn't know. there was that
night that i sat with her in a darkened room, facing
her, staring intensely at her lovely invisibility. she
was perfectly silent and i heard what she said. i
reached out and touched her hair.
i stroked it.

she said "please don't" and i withdrew my hand.
later i went abroad. tugged by chains of curiosity, he
took my place in the tinsel, in the sawdust, in the
phosphorescent glare of the palace of eviscerated
dreams and she evened the score with somebody just
to keep the record straight. i saw them years later
and they were sad. she said to me "that evening long
ago, did you look at me in the darkness, did you
stroke my hair or did i just imagine it?" she asked
me that and she looked at me with longing. "yes, i
touched you," i answered, "i loved you then." she
lowered her eyes and said, "oh."

he painted the harbor

he painted the harbor. he painted the harbor & the
neighbors said he was a crazy old man. puffed out
sailor. dilettante. what a way to spend a retirement. he
painted the harbor. he'd never been to art school and
they called him a self-styled painter, a puffed out sailor
and a crazy old man but he painted the harbor. he
painted the harbor on whatever pieces of flotsam he
could find. he couldn't afford canvas and maybe he
didn't care so he painted on old cardboard boxes and
broken up pieces of wood and whatever else was laying
around and they kept saying he was odd and kept to
himself and there he was in his little cottage painting
away and painting the harbor and that proved he was
peculiar and just a crazy old man just a puffed out sailor,
wasting his retirement, having airs in his old age. he
painted the harbor. he painted the harbor and no one
exhibited his work. he painted the harbor and no one
bought a painting. he painted the harbor and covered the
walls of his little cottage with paintings and no one came
to see. he painted the harbor. he painted the harbor until
one day he died. and as he left nothing of value and as
he had no heirs and no one who cared, his landlord took
his paintings and no one noticed. he was just a corpse
that used to paint the harbor. and then one day – i don't
know why – maybe because he was dead – maybe
because he was dead and nobody had to talk to him, he
became a cult. most of his neighbors still said he was a
crazy old man but his artist neighbors said he was great
and his other neighbors just remembered a crazy old man
and felt they were being had and if he was so great why
hadn't his artist neighbors said so when he was still
alive. he was just a retired sailor. just a crazy puttering
puffed out old sailor who didn't talk to you or go to the
pub and mind his place like ordinary people but put on

airs and had pretensions by doing crazy things like painting the harbor. and a famous artist, sort of a neighbor, who had been a critic for a major newspaper, who was influential and knew a lot of big people and knew a lot of big words and who painted big canvasses with big circles on them, well not exactly circles, but sort of lumpy circles in bright colors that hung in the most important private art gallery in the country, well he came down to the crazy old sailor's cottage and made a speech about how the crazy old sailor was a great artist and everyone who was anybody believed him because his lumpy circles were internationally famous and the mayor was there and the circle painter betrayed the cause of art by not strangling the mayor on the spot but instead using words and phrases and ideas the crazy old man would never have understood and would have spat on while he painted his harbors, and a stone was unveiled, set high up in the wall of the cottage, honoring the old man, giving his name and the dates of his life and saying he had lived in this cottage and that he was an artist and mariner. and his cottage became a museum and his paintings were hung in it and other paintings were loaned by his landlord to the local art society, the well established former revolutionary local art society which had had nothing to do with the crazy old man while he was still alive, wouldn't talk to the crazy old man, but now graciously thanked his landlord who had expropriated his paintings, graciously thanked him and hung this painted flotsam and jetsam on its hallowed walls. and i don't know whether the crazy old sailor ever guessed that all of this would happen. all i know is this: he painted the harbor.

to my month-old daughter on the conditions of greatness

you're great. you're great because you are. just because you exist that is. you are great for drawing breath, for turning your head & beginning to see the world, for taking nourishment, for moving, for being, for that inarticulate burble & that involuntary smile. you are great for your cry is the quintessential poetry of all anguish. you are great for your innocence is a shorthand for the innocence of us all. your grandeur is no delusion. for many thousands of years <u>you</u> have been a religion. strangers welcome you. billions of wise men and fools. there are those who do not but they are a minority. those who are disturbed by your piercing poetry, whom it makes nervous. there are even those who may belittle your beauty in the name of your excrement which you yourself take for granted with that magnificent neutrality which has neither discovered revulsion nor the need to know that this is a building block of living. the precise meaning of my words is exquisitely irrelevant to you. you are the ideal poetry audience for all you care about is the warmth of the sound & you have your own urgencies that transcend even that. you're great. you're beautiful. you're beautiful for just being. you <u>always</u> will be. & just because you happen to grow up & people foolishly withdraw the welcome which you accepted in the best of faith ... well hear this now: you're great. and don't you ever forget it.

browsing in an antiquarian bookshop

i am drawn here by intellectual maggotry, the smell of old books
& decaying knowledge. all this dead literature, corseted in
morocco binding. all these shattered hypotheses, mummified in
the name of immortality. the book-seller is pathologically honest.
"this is sheer rubbish," she says. and again, "would you read
carlyle?" long ago in my own ancient past i used to read dickens.
even had a harmless flirtation with dostoevsky. was hoodwinked
by byron about the time i pubesced. they sell batteries and fruit
in the marketplace & both have to be reasonably new but this is a
store for used-up books. there is something here of the wonder
that filled my childhood with romantic rusty boilers and esoteric
coils in vacant lots, that enamored me of obscure graph papers in
stationery stores on canal street, that drew me to country
tombstones. here is the mystical source of the value of antiques.
here is edgar allan poe dancing with virginia a waltz with
undertones of necrophilia.
here lie the remnants of a bygone culture.
may they rest in peace.

the appointment

> the pleasure you will experience in
> discovering truth will repay you for your
> work; don't expect other compensation,
> because it may not come. Yet dare."
> -- immanuel velikovsky

on the broken bones of all the men who are me

there is a citadel whose walls i have to scale

that rises on a hill above the blood-filled sea

there is a man inside its dungeon as in jail

another man whose freedom may be fated

another me who's trapped inside that wall

who with this engine may be liberated

who then is he? how many years in thrall?

& what if the handles on that door are polished?

& what if when i scaled the wall i slipped?

& what if the citadel or more has been demolished?

& what if all the grapples have been shipped

away to kali only to disarm her?

& what if all approaches are on fire?

& what if all my freedom songs alarm her?

& what if on the threshold i expire?

the me that's on the other side

of walls & clocks may not have much to teach

& yet he is a mystery, an enigma, i'll confide

i'd suffer half eternity to reach

principia poetica

"home is where the book is"
- bernard malamud

what is this rock they're all demolishing

why are they tearing the world apart

why does the foreman stand there polishing

a fistful of granite that he calls his heart

why are they hacking away at the mountain

where did they get those picks they're employing

ten thousand men for one lousy fountain

one cup of water from all they're destroying

a bent rusty nail to puncture the can

a stone for a hammer to build them a shower

soot on the face of the one-armed man

who in one ray of sunshine will water the flower

the wilted old flower on the dusty old road

that dreams of the rivers & whispers of seas

that's watered by virtue of hills that explode

& all of them sinais & all calvaries

but what is this rock that they're all demolishing

why are they tearing the world apart

they scream & they strain as the foreman stands polishing

a fistful of granite and calls it his heart

<u>the tabernacles of the robbers prosper</u>

(title from the book of job)

never mind how god let himself be hyped by a trivial
theological discussion with satan into ripping job off
and tormenting him and his family.
the point of that parable, tho monstrous, is clear
enough. but what about ... well, consider the starting
point where satan says to god who he hangs around
with, hey well, why shouldn't job dig you when
you've laid such groovies on him - large flocks,
gigantic treasury, a season ticket to 3 mile island?
god had, according to the story, originally provided
well for job in exchange for his piety –
a calvinist god that week he was. but what about ...
the fortunes & powers & adoration heaped upon the
greatest villains of time? where in the book of job,
the koran, the mahabharata or anywhere else does it
explain the ethical logic of <u>that</u>?
or what philosophical point
the creator was then trying - for whatever reason -
to get across to his wicked assistant?

<u>stone handkerchief, a true fable</u>

once upon a time there was a house in which no one lived.

the house was meant as a repository for the disembodied spirit

of the entire universe, a force that was supposed to be moral.

the house was torn down & many of the descendants

of the builders of the house were tortured & murdered.

these torments were so terrible that some of the survivors

needed a place to cry. bulldozers were called in

to knock down the houses of the impoverished people

(of another nation) who lived near the house

where no one lived - people who now had nowhere to live.

so one set of victims evicted another set of victims

in order to have a place to cry

concerning their own victimisation -

a place that was a remnant of the house where

no one had ever lived.

they call that remnant the wailing wall.

the doors behind you are closed

(title by kurt vonnegut)

trash like the iliad or the brothers karamazov never
goes out of print. other books may have their season,
only to flower and perish, usually well before the author
dies. that's the way it is with the office politics of time.
consider mistakes as a class of events. mine. yours.
everyone's. if a somewhat different turning had been
taken here or here or here, if just one piece of
information had arrived when it was still timely, might
we not have been worse off after all? there's little
i know of any value that was not learned on a burning
bridge or a sinking ship. when precisely was it that
the passengers on the titanic discovered that formal dress
was irrelevant? less to the point, at what juncture in
human history did rasputin's psychotherapist give up
smoking? there, that's what i mean ... had lucidity
arrived just then, that line would never have been
written. there's no time to change it now. if those
are really strategic bombers up above, even the iliad may
go out of print.

<u>to a dead mouse</u>

why that eternity look in the slightly bulging eyes
below the crushed skull, oh you in the trap and why
this testimonial from your executioner who could not
even poetry for his own dead father rotting still on
the gallows of time having been hurled there by the
same dynamic that imprisons us all and why my self-
justifying feelings, talk of food-poisoning and of the
long walk in the rain today to get to town to give to
errant humanity my blood in the echoes of which to
wash my alienated soul - you, mouse, this is to you,
small invader on tiny spring-action crucifix carrying
the retribution of those who hurl me into the outer
reaches of space and drag me naked into courts of
civil inquisition - you, virgin mouse, who would
rather have retained life and freedom than, rigid in
the doom of evening, to have inspired this dirty
poem.

bitch on wheels

on the one hand, the frozen gibberish, the reticent scholars with
their icy fingers, the apotheosis of zombies, the learned vampires
wearing the rancid perfume of dead poetry, the phoney concept
artists, the new wave, the fraudulent classicism of jagged gears,
the dancing bears, the clique of the living dead.

on the other hand, the fire on the hill, the blackened greenery, the
farmer like don quixote, beating helplessly at the burning bush as
the entire landscape melts into something like powdered tar - grey
upon black - symbol of spent fury of inarticulate pyromanic anti-
intellectual doom.

there was another place once - a swampy moorland some miles
from here where a viscount pulled me through the marsh like a
toy on a string. i lost my glasses in the muck - got bifocals - saw
better as a result.

it is dark now. perhaps the fire is dying.

fevers rage. primitive plumbing splutters.

there is plenty of room for anger.

<u>your bill</u>

over the edge of the knife of hunger

exists another world

beyond the locus of love songs

are torments devised by pol pot

amin, da vinci, hitler, croesus

over the edge & beyond the capacity of poetry

worlds

in which sparrow chirps are irrelevant

worlds in which

all my words would decay

where none of my formulae would be valid

worlds in which it wouldn't matter

if your painting disintegrated

or if your symphony was ever composed

the only music here

the scream

the moan

and finally the silence

the manifesto of the dying child

<u>written in the rain</u>
<u>while walking home</u>
<u>from a neighboring village</u>

(for marie claude pace)

and whether beneath

    the slate sky

the bricks like north & north

or south & south

of the tower of babel

    repel each other

the attempt to build the tower

is nevertheless

despite myth & perversion

holy

& if we collapse

in a pile of rubble

& broken language

if the old man on the bicycle to henry's bridge

does not speak -

the rosebuds

on the twigs strapped to his luggage rack

will anyhow open in the rain

a love letter to the wind

i am a lover of the wind. i breathe in short breaths
heavily as the wind carries me away into
    the turmoil of existence
the redemptive disquietude of my disorderly soul.
i ride with the wind through the fires it whips into
    cauterizing fury
the waters it raises up, the clouds it shatters
the earth itself that it disgorges from her nest.
i make love to the melody of the wind
am disconcerted as it doffs my hat
as it stirs my hair and spirit
as it challenges categorically the system of my dreams.
the wind is metaphor and it is itself
cross-pollinator of lives and revolutions
ancient motor of sailing ships, invisible angel of death
the wave upon which will ride the dandelion seed
the barometric symphony, the transpersonification of excitement
- i compose my odes to the wind on the backs of invoices
and with uncritical appreciation
the wind will carry them away ...

<u>the origin of jacob's ladder</u>

(for tony & olive west)

electric violet at the edge of the field

magnetic drawing the wild bee to it ...

here, the pain of near-silence -

of avalanching compacted time

a half-century of a particular journey

drawing to its ultimate

and exceedingly dangerous distillation ---

what is the statue that stands at the intersection

of numbness avenue and passion boulevard? ---

i set out to tell the story of my life in a few words

this morning

and a letter arrived telling me my friend is leaving -

me a somewhat woodwormed ladder

that with care & repair

will enable me to touch the sun ...

in return i give him this tiny poem

<u>the siege</u>

it is not the gypsies who steal your children.
it is not even the education authorities, the army recruiting
officers, the sinister saints of television.
your children are being stolen by automatons –
by well-meaning or unmeaning, unthinking
agents of sordid socialisation ...
those unlettered little old ladies, for instance, who jump out
from behind the hedges – confront your toddler and say
"going to school heh heh heh?" these are the intergalactic
truancy patrol ... those friendly men who show your kid
their medals or their queen victoria coronation chamber pot –
you must wall your child with love & silence & words
against these guilty innocents
who steal the gypsies' children.

<u>semi-orthogonal variation on a line by jacob bush</u>

how then would you spend your life

if all those useless tasks that bear the names of commerce &

   industry – religiosity & litigation – bureaucracy & politics

if all those ...

if the women were not to embrace these ephemera

abandoning the milling of flour & other fulfilling pursuits

     we men might envy

to wear the scrip chains of ostensible liberation

     in the electronic factory of our synthetic soul

if all ...

if the children instead of being schooled in brutality

     exuberated their boundless energies

     leaping over rainbows - annotating in lavender

     deep philosophy

     the girls wearing geraniums in their hair

     the boys draping marigolds over the clouds

if ...

how then would you spend your life

if the entire foundation of the human experience as we know it

were to be shattered in a sequence

     of random felt-tipped technicolored entries

     in the time sheet of god knows what - - - - -

gloriously irrelevant endeavor

medieval rhapsody

he painted on the surface of the muddy brook itself
as the clouded waters ebbed & flowed & paid
their uncertain tribute to the river

a lady in timeless robes
riding a horse of all colors
paused by the edge of the brook
& asked him why he labored so
& for so many years decorated a parchment
that edged its way into the sea

he answered that her words changed meaning as she spoke
that his brush died with each stroke
that the universe as it existed a moment ago
as she arrived on this shore
was no more

he told her that the only truth in her song -
was the music

<u>it is our solemn duty</u>

"it is our solemn duty
to bury the dead"
--- british chaplain at
a mass grave for
argentinean soldiers

it is our solemn duty

it is our solemn duty to bury the dead

it is our solemn duty to support our respective

establishments

and provide them with military chaplains

and fortify professional killers in delusions of

religiosity

it is our solemn duty to march with the troops

to minister to their psyches and

with sophisticated weaponry

to transform the faulted living

into the irreproachable dead

so that at last we may discharge our duty to them

and in the name of a merciful god ...

bury the youthful dead

the explanation of evil

(to the memory of my friend, butch newland
a twenty year old black civil rights
trade union and peace activist
murdered in new york city in 1950)

> "i don't know who makes the
> laws of that slip knot"
> - woody guthrie

the explanation of the evil that has befallen you
      is that in a previous life you earned
      negative merit which is why the deity
      positioned you in auschwitz or nagasaki
      which is to say you and your fellow victims
      were more wicked than most before you started,
      more wicked perhaps than your tormentors
      (and therefore shouldn't be rescued)

the explanation of the evil that has befallen you
      is that god loves you and is testing you
      and that's why he's starving you in the desert
      because he nailed his own son to the sky
      because he loves the head of the chase
      manhattan bank less and so abuses him less
      and he lovingly gave you free will
      so why the hell aren't you eating?

the explanation of the evil that has befallen you
      is that it's all just the luck of the draw
      all just part of a larger plan
      that genuine justice would be boring
      that you're just passing through
      and things will be wonderful when you're dead

the explanation of the evil that has befallen you
  is that the physical world is unreal
  is that everything is a playful illusion
  including your screams at the stake
  and your gasps on the dunking stool
  and that god is just a jolly sadistic joker
  and in any case has an entire universe
  to manage and no time for you

the explanation of the evil that has befallen you
  is that it is a blessing in disguise
  that your ten years in gulag
  or on a new mexico chain gang
  are meant to purify and refine your spirit
  and not make you small and narrow and dictatorial
  and vengeful and the other things that
  tortured souls too often seem to become -
  that suffering, in fact, is a privilege

the explanation of the evil that has befallen you
  is that it's god's will, that he has a hidden purpose
  and moves in mysterious ways, that the omnipotent one
  can't intervene, that the central committee hasn't met
  that you chose your womb poorly, that desire is the
  cause of all your suffering so follow the eightfold
  path and do not long for the cessation or abatement
  of the bicycle chain crashing across your face

the explanation of the evil that has befallen you
  is that, empirical bruises & accolades to the contrary,
  what you do is said by witches & levites
  to rebound on you

the explanation of the evil that has befallen you
  and of your eviscerated body - is counterpoint,
  is that the real revolution if such there be
  is yet to come and meanwhile
  saintly inquisitors explain
  the origins of evil

the explanation of the evil that has befallen you
  is that there is no explanation
  of the evil that has befallen you

cancellation

"not to go where one can go
would be subversive."
- - ivan d. illich

remove the bejeweled wheels of the caravan
spokes of sunshine encrusted with the mud
of far-off exotic swamps,
                    hang the wheels low
in some obscure & humble sky
                        over some forgotten
or never known
                hamlet on the reverse of the one-sided surface ...
you could have done no better than to scratch one corner
        of the cosmos,
                    than to have heard a few notes of the many
        read a few lines
                    unless
in burning your shoes
                    in a dung fire
                            in the black night
while faltering reflections of erratic starlight
    dart between the patches of mud on the bejeweled wheels
        of the dismantled caravan
                    you find in the wisps of nearly invisible smoke
every infinity of time, space & those things
        that transcend imagination
                that ever in the now or later
                    or might have been
                            was

an epitaph for noreen

teach, teach me something
she said and, soon after, died
hear the brown earth sing

what can wise men bring
when everything's been tried
teach, teach me something

hail the nettle sting
hail the sky so very wide
hear the brown earth sing

though the fool be king
the uni-verse is defied
teach, teach me something

rust will close the ring
and there is no need to hide
hear the brown earth sing

she of shattered wing
almost as an aside, said
reach, teach me something
teach me, hear the brown earth sing
listen ... listen ... hear it sing

<u>take two</u>

he painted the harbor. he came home from the sea to be
with his wife and his wife died and he painted the harbor.
he wore the town like an overcoat and huddled in his
cottage and tore up cardboard boxes onto which he painted
the harbor. he hung his paintings outside the cottage and
he painted the harbor. and overprivileged artists saw them
and bought packets of paintings for pennies and imitated
them and passed them around to their friends to imitate
and, as art is corrupt, their fame grew and his diminished
and he painted the harbor. and he died in the work house
and as he was dead and as he had no eyes to read, within a year
or two one of his talented penny patrons paid "tribute"
by writing about him and now he is known all over the world
and generates folk tales. still, he painted the harbor.

<u>determinant in blank verse</u>

and well beyond the world of walls and clocks
beneath the pain the joy the deep fatigue
beyond reach of critical corrosion
within impressionistic memory
rain blurred watercolors on frosted glass
do not teach but can only reinforce
rhythms already here so long ago
when not yet in the maze but manacled
while in the cage with beating heart and wings
he bayed in moonlight at the burning stars

epilogue

"what if your life itself
became a poem?"
- - caroline of cornwall

the vandals arrived the day after the edifice had been completed.
this puzzled him as its completion had not been announced and as
it had none of the attractions of solomon's temple, none of that
kind of ostentation, no gilded cherubs, platinum bulls, sun at
solstice trepanating the silver and ebony buddha at pineal ruby,
no pathology of confirmation, unicorn tapestries on prison walls,
no berlioz. the structure, in fact, was in an isolated glen whistling
quietly with stagnant whirlwinds trapped aeons ago when
ambivalent troglodytes conjured from the 12th dimension of an
11-dimensional reality had excavated here for lead to transmute
into even more lethal gold. the structure was made of inobtrusive
slabs of slate and planks of consciousness, less inelegant than an
armory, less austere than a methodist chapel, yet as quiet as a
poem which is to say as scarcely audible as a secret shouted from
a rooftop, and yet, in the absence of any publicity, the vandals,
uncomprehending and wearing blindfolds, swooped down upon
the edifice as instinctually as a gypsy moth separated from his
lover by hundreds of miles, and with their battering rams made
cracks in the most ancient cornerstones. he had been able to
photograph the building before it fell and considered this to be of
unearthly value. he wept, of course. eventually he shrugged.
"what's a life work between friends, or even enemies?" he said.
the cracks, after all, had been preordained by perverse destiny and
hyperboloid radio loops. his time nearly expired, generating no
words for mortar this time, post-pharaonic, free and solitary,
having no staff, no diagrams and no schemata, with the wrong
tools, yet armed with stochastic serendipity and ingesting the
fluorescent hieroglyphs of others, in a contracting and therefore
essential world, burning still with the fire that does not consume,
turning himself on the wheel,,,,, he began again.

<u>o happy grief</u>

(title by w.h. auden)

                     the grass hut in the arctic tundra, the
steel staves of the gate, like upended harpoons,
bearing frozen skulls grinning into the biting wind.
my low hum inside the hut, signifying that resolutions
are literary artifacts, yet answering the cry of the gale
outside that magically does not dismantle the structure
wherein I sit nursing my broken vow. the other
sounds that penetrate, lace, sew my concentration to
the wall, pierce my imagination with the
electromagnetic coda of
my forever waylaid person. hot buffalo milk
and betrayal by sympathetic listeners.
ten thousand spiders and as many parlors.
the churches with their broken crosses.
the first aid stations with their red swastikas.
fraudulent rebels walking streets paved with
conformity. warehouses stuffed with clichés.
the tyranny of everyday life

POETRY FOR PEACE

with

PAT VON TWEST • JACOB BUSH
Buskers Anonymous • Folk Music
and yet more verbiage

CLWB IFOR BACH, WOMANBY STREET (Opposite the Castle), CARDIFF
SATURDAY NIGHT, AUGUST 8th, 8.30 p.m. - 2. a.m. (Late Bar)

TICKETS / TOCYNNAU £2.00 UNWAGED £1.50

FROM THE PEACE STALL, MACKINTOSH PLACE, OR CARAVAN

PROCEEDS TO / ER BUDD : MOLESWORTH, PEACE PLEDGE UNION, AND CND

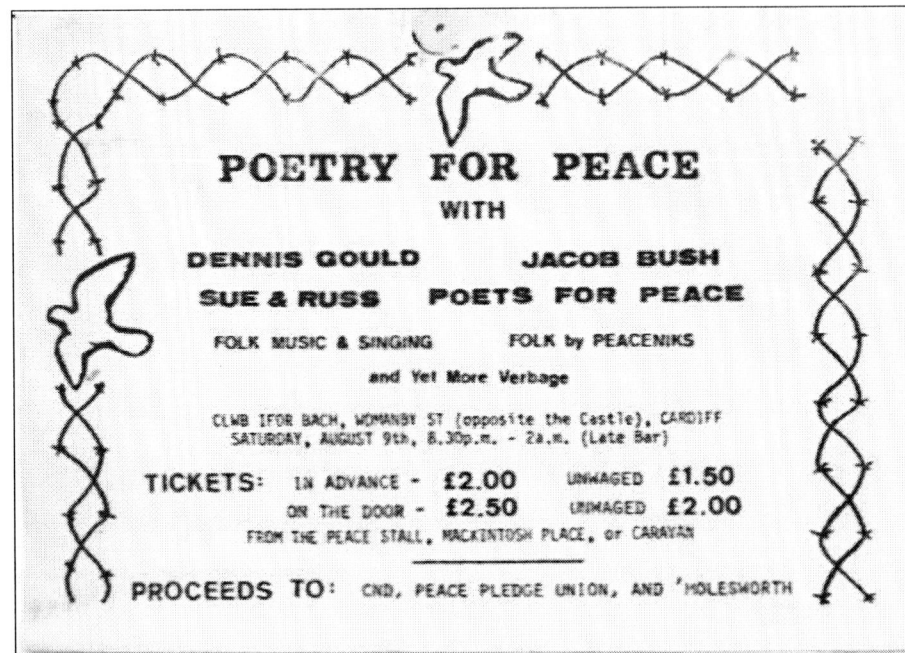

POETRY FOR PEACE
WITH

DENNIS GOULD   JACOB BUSH

SUE & RUSS   POETS FOR PEACE

FOLK MUSIC & SINGING   FOLK by PEACENIKS

and Yet More Verbage

CLWB IFOR BACH, WOMANBY ST (opposite the Castle), CARDIFF
SATURDAY, AUGUST 9th, 8.30p.m. - 2a.m. (Late Bar)

TICKETS: IN ADVANCE - £2.00   UNWAGED £1.50
          ON THE DOOR - £2.50   UNWAGED £2.00
FROM THE PEACE STALL, MACKINTOSH PLACE, or CARAVAN

PROCEEDS TO: CND, PEACE PLEDGE UNION, AND 'MOLESWORTH

reflection

> "Thine eyes shall see,
>   God's image in the glass
> I send to thee."
>   - HAFIZ
>   (from the 7th ode)

ancient mirror whose silver's worn away

   broken glass admitting rain, wind and sun

at forest edge where dried out rivers run

   where masking rhythms heighten what we say

as tao te ching declines to tell the way

   the nazarene declines to load his gun

eternal day will still have not begun

   long after all these words have blown away

seeking myself i lift the mirror high

   and 'neath the cloudy sky i peer and stare

into the ancient glass before me here

   my eyes do not deceive nor senses lie

when gazing through the glass i see you there

your face so sad, so beautiful, so dear

variations on a passage from the book of changes

"the superior man in his conduct exceeds in humility"

by exceeding in humility, he demonstrates his superiority

    since the book of changes says it is the superior man

    who exceeds in humility

by demonstrating his superiority, the superior man

    proves his arrogance

the superior man in his humility exceeds in arrogance

the superior man, in consulting the book of changes,

    demonstrates his non-superiority, as the book

    is addressed to the superior man and, thinking himself

    superior, he lacks in humility

thus, the humble man, being superior, does not

    consult the book of changes

failing to consult the book of changes, the humble

    man does not read the above passage

unless, of course, he reads its transcription

    by an inferior man arrogant enough

    to argue with the dead

torn corner of a fading photograph

"the music took us some strange places ...
physically, spiritually and psychotically"
- robbie robertson

this is the house where the music lives

where the stars are whirling & the universe dies

and the demon drinks what the angel gives

and the chandelier tears holes in the skies

where the madam from the shanty town

and the sacred clown of articulate madness

build babel while tearing old jericho down

while painting with sunlight the shrine of their sadness

here at the house where ego street

and the avenue of god ...

meet

a short celebration of sadness

tchaikovski switched off the television. those old
1945 fred allen movies laboring unfunny with their
grasping greed and undialectical materialism
(so characteristic of the patriotic war) brought him
down. fred allen, for his part, egoistically life-
affirming, just reached out of the cathode screen,
turned the knob and reactivated his sordid persona.
tchaikovski, wearing darkness like an illuminated
cloak, drew the protective night around his
shoulders, sat down at his invisible piano, and
composed the pathétique.

<u>nocturne</u>

the tinkling of small change in my pocket
gave offense to your somber forest
    it being night, a multitude of stars were visible
    excepting twin suns, each one solitary
i remember the quiet back road and the chapel at the edge
the hymns being in welsh, we didn't understand the words
which made the music somehow more comprehensible
    yes, you are right... i <u>was</u> angry
    i walked away, defeated, having tried
    to apprehend your phrases with my mind
afterwards, naturally, my heart understood

<u>the big bang</u>

> "My work consists of two parts:
> the one presented here and all
> that I have <u>not</u> written. And
> it is precisely the second part
> that is the important one."
>
> - ludwig wittgenstein

it's when you cast off your divining rods

and disencumber yourself divesting

geomancy and guttman scaling

time series and tarot decks

factor analyses & charts of tide & moon phases

restore to the rabbit his severed foot

disgorge the stock quotations

the twin curses of vindication & revenge

the electronic catatonia & fibre-optic technocratic populism

the ballots, bullets, barometrics, bombs

deeds, diplomas, prescriptions

actuarial tables & cost-of-living indices

poetry competitions and other contradictions in terms

scientism, sinecures, sycophancy & intellectual mafiosi

academic swamp water reconstituting distilled literature & art

triumphant utopias inexorably gone wrong,

symphonic delusions

sadly granted wishes, success wreaths, finality & industry

droppings of paid vultures feeding on the

       visions of affluent paupers

genetically engineered disasters and

       erudite faustian hooliganism

frozen rage, explanations, prayers,

       soul surgeons, spirit transplants

incantations, musical notations, states, nations, multinationals

community and fashionable clothing

and stand naked on some barren asteroid

and knot with a whimper the rope of no matter

plummeting through a near vacuum

ascending past icarus with his backpack

shivering freezing wailing incomprehensible

uncomprehendingly beyond all theory

structure pigmentation or texture of sound –

that the freedom, the terror

the nervous emancipating anxiety

worth ten thousand dead tranquilities

BEGINS

<u>point at infinity</u>

the point, said marx, is not to study society but to change it.
the point is not the dissemination of culture but its
transformation, the laser-shattering of moldy mythology's
homogenizing visions. the point is the resuscitation of subtlety,
the other side of ecstasy. the point is the poverty of wealth, the
impotence of power, the blessed impossibility of security.
it is we, with the empty pockets, who have all the risk capital.
imagine stockhausen reflecting modern life at some medieval dig
where sinister monks are excavating the thermonuclear bones of
homer while adoring peasants and noblemen sing songs of praise
and you have imagined the fuse that extends to the core of the
explosive existence or otherwise of our world. imagine
conchobar with blood-stained fingers leafing through illuminated
fanzines in the library at alexandria. the point is not to describe
but to circumscribe, not to resurrect ancient heroes but to bury
them, not renaissance but liberation, not universities but
universes, nothing short of dialectical immaterialism of the tiniest
light in the remotest corner enveloping, incorporating, washing
with freedom the elegantly tragic whole.

allegory

nevertheless, the universe

despite the golden bullet sweeping out

an elegant vista as it trepanned rainbows through

the red waterfall it created in his brain

fired through the tunnelled vision

computer barrel into this is not the future

nor the higher evolution which is the child of entropy

beyond life forms

an explication of iterative pantheons ...

he died

standing alone

not having spoken,,,,

the imperishable, unconquerable all-permeating

reality he perceived

by his death rendered occult –

awaiting your rediscovery

direct from the source

take three

he painted the harbor. he was a junk man who
never smoked opium and he painted the harbor.
he was a fisherman, a sailor, an ice cream vendor,
a widower who painted the harbor. he was not
fashionably educated, a genuine holy pauper amidst
the pseudo-poverty of synthetic saints. he was not
a suicide. being poor, he knew the wealth of life.
with the erudition of his viscera, he recognised
in their minimalism, the attempt to sum up
the cosmic symphony in a fart. he considered
abandoning his paints, felt victimised by persecution and
jealousy, persevered, died penniless, buried
not in a potter's field but beneath a potter's tombstone.
he painted the harbor. when others were staring at the
harbor and painting the void, he painted the harbor.
the harbor!

on a london bus

(the phrase, "as wheels in water,"
was proposed by anthony c. west,
who suggested i write a sonnet
incorporating it.)

as wheels in water, as the pharaoh drowns
as water flows, as only oceans see
at ganges' mouth, as seas destroy the towns
the verse must fathom whether it should be.

as angels fathom whether they must fly
as mad pneumatic heartbeats crack the ground
the singer ponders whether she should die
her song reduced to that staccato sound.

each question answered yields one question more
each answer questioned withers in the rain
the culture barge boat heaps upon the shore
a gravel made of ego ground with pain

and shall we melt the snow into a brook
to trap between the covers of a book?

(anthony c. west died
nov. 19th, 1988; this
poem is dedicated to
him & his writing.)

<u>parable</u>

moses sat on the promontory and scratched his head.
he was an old man and his memory was going. he couldn't
remember what precisely had been the sin that disqualified
him from leading these people into the land below. it
hadn't been <u>he</u> who had fashioned the calf: he could
remember that. and yet <u>they</u> were not disqualified from
going.
what was it now that made joshua so worthy?
there were advance press releases going out that he played a
mean trumpet but then it was whispered that he couldn't
build and could only take that which was already standing.
moses sighed. being allowed to see the land was a mixed
blessing after all. but then he was an old man. he had done
a lot of walking ... had to watch his cholesterol count.
what the hell did he want with milk and honey?

shard

her coat was black, with sunshine lined

and in her eye a cloud rolled by

her wisps of hair were ill-defined

i think her mind contained the sky

she wafted slowly through my dream

and then she floated back again

and said, "the flowers that you see

contain the captured souls of men."

the salvation of oedipus

oedipus leaned back in the taxi and tried to smoke one of those
herbal cigarettes they sell in the health food shop, the kind they
make of coltsfoot and honey. it burned his throat and he crushed
it in the ashtray in the back of the driver's seat. there was no
driver which was strange because the car was zooming down
jericho turnpike and although uranus had turned on his side in the
heavens, wounded by the politics of cronus, the cab was not out
of control. oedipus, ever aware of doom, radiant with
chernobylity, leafed through a well-worn paperback of sophocles,
intent on finding out what was to happen next. as a boy he had,
through family connections, always obtained the may issue of
blue beetle comics the preceding march and so had developed a
taste for divination. he glanced up at the meter whose drachmas
of the spirit already exceeded, in violation of even the most
radical theories and conceptualizations, the first transfinite
cardinal number. the self-propelled cab slowed down and pulled
over to a lay-by. oedipus got out, fetched some equipment from
the glove compartment, painted the vehicle scarlet with a gorse-
gold stripe, got back in and waited until it started again. he
leaned back, lit another of those coltsfoot things and inhaled
deeply. with the strange contentment of the condemned, he
contemplated the fare.

going in

> "i will cultivate within
> me scrupulously the
> Inimitable which
> is loneliness ..."
> - e.e.cummings

in beyond the snares of memory
in beyond the deceptions of past
in through the chaos
into the still point at the center
burrowing into the giant stone
past the dead figures of sunshine
past the shadows that pass for people
past measures, calibrations, skin
in beyond the illness
in beyond salvation
in beyond certainty
into the valley of shattered clocks
in
past nation
belief
into the soul of music
into the river of tears
laughter
weakness
softness
victory
in

to become a writer

to become a writer, you must first stop writing. you must go to dinner parties and teach courses, build a thousand foot wall around your house to insulate yourself from hadrian's barbarians. you must use pneumatic drills to install proustian wallpaper, thus safeguarding your ears against the onslaught of the hurricane within. you must ride a raft down the yangtze and live in a barrel in niagara falls, raise a family, wear a garter belt, hide in a monastery and cultivate your soul. to become a writer, you must run out of ink, you must shred your typewriter ribbons with razor blades, you must invite castration in the marketplace, scream elegantly in the halls of power, forfeit power thereby achieving it, be humble yet arrogant. to become a writer, you must take a line like, "to become a writer, you must first stop writing," pull it out of the air that is yourself, nurture it for sixteen years in hidden places, while you go about your business, shopping, filling in forms, pulling poisoned darts out of your temples, and then dash off some words about it for sixteen minutes, and read them at sixteen poetry readings. then you will be a writer at last, even though you were already a writer even before you wrote. it is another matter to escape. you may not escape through writing. writing is going in, escape is going out. you may however hide inside the envelope that you mail to a foreign publisher and thus evade the border guards of consciousness. if you're lucky, you might go insane. to become a writer you must first feed the hungry and burn your money and fall in love with the truth. to become a writer, you must first ... stop writing.

on seeing an army of bicyclists
crossing a bridge on the river taf

a few
more
many
a break in traffic
more
another break and still they come
round and round the seasons of the wheels
up the city boulevard ...
myself when young did
ride alone –
my bicycle my horse –
on elegantly lonely journeys
to ocean waves, to urban woods
to wordless conversations with a silent god ...
but here is an army
reactionary as armies must be ...
a few more
many more
many many more ...
i look out the window
and up the quiet street
that leads to the boulevard ...
in scarcely explicable terror

<u>to be caught unawares</u>

and so be unprepared
and live the unexpected moment
in non-pre-emptive openness

i knew a man once who insured his house
against lightning ...
the flood carried it away –
another bought a rowboat ...
his farm became a desert

too much preparedness
leaves no time for that
for which you prepare

sleep, awake ...
rub your eyes –
it is no fun to take a bath
in a suit of armor

we all die
what can be lost
by barricading your castle
with dreaming?

<u>the work itself</u>

into the flame to freedom
into the flame to the heart of the moon
the moth itself the fog
into the fog the heart of the flame
into the dying tosca-born century
into the salty rain
into pandora's restaurant for european pie
into the sacré coeur
where the churchwarden sews with red thread
gold tassel on the twin black banners
of anarchy and death
into painful memories
of childhood and crucifixion
into fiction transcending fact
to poetry and back
through the sinews of music
through bartok's boogie tears
into the soul of rumi
through mosque synagogue temple and pagoda
into the melchite church where saints lay down their arms
into the windowsill flowerpots where the geraniums grow
into the sky
to a distant planet called earth
into birth
and freedom

pantun fifty-four

in the sacred wilderness of the soul
where the tall tower has never been built
here in dead ruins where hot oceans roll
here transcendent birds rise up from the silt

where the tall tower has never been built
where pterodactyls ring the golden sun
here transcendent birds rise up from the silt
here the uncommenceable is begun

where pterodactyls ring the golden sun
here in hot ruins where dead oceans roll
here the uncommenceable is begun
in the sacred wilderness of the soul

newly discovered fragment of an aesopian manuscript

the fox, having been a liberal sociologist in a previous incarnation, reflected further and on mature consideration concluded that, undoubtedly, the grapes must have been sweet after all. not wishing to be vulpemorphic or self-serving in his mode of thought, he was prepared to admit that that which was beyond his reach was indeed the most desirable prize after all. later that same day, however, the pasture being greener, a strong gust of wind and one fortuitous deus ex machina crack of lightning severed the branch supporting the vine, and a cluster of the grapes came tumbling into the edge of the delightful stream from which the fox was, at that very moment, drinking. with hardly any more reflection, but after uttering the fox equivalent of grace, the creature began eating the grapes. soon after, he vomited. he had consumed them all, you see, unwilling to admit that, in fact, they really were sour.

<u>beyond myself</u>

"what surer sign
than the seeker
after the sign?"
-rumi

i am a particular moving matrix of perceptual modes
among the sparrows and the hawkweeds and the
aquamarine cottons fluttering in the forgetful wind of
foreverness, my tormented intestines the strings of a
hypercelestial cello participating in the unwritten
symphonies of the jazz of the lost books of jasher, my
back straightened, straining against the weight of
eternity, my breath, tumultuous, frosting the window
panes, transcending the frames of space, flowering,
crystalline blossoms shattered in the blinding
particularization of individuated pain,
recoalescing in the self that is beyond self, freed while
yet imprisoned in aspiration, the message that needs
no telling.

<u>creation myth</u>

long ago, but not beyond recall,

this agate of event horizons

tunnelled through one of the singularities

in one of the numberless mountains

in the range of the not quite all - -

and tears were shed

vaster than imaginings

for both the ecstasies and the torments

of all that had to be ...

over fifteen billion years ago,

when athena's contractions began

WRITERS' HOLIDAY SHOWCASE '87

presenting

Phil Carradice

Francesca Kay

Jacob Bush

Carl Tighe

*being held at
The Caerleon Centre on
Thursday 6 August
commencing 8·00pm. Bar. Disco to 1·00.*
free admission

IN ASSOCIATION WITH THE SOUTH EAST WALES ARTS ASSOCIATION THE WELSH ACADEMY AND THE WELSH ARTS COUNCIL

<u>for my own dead father</u>

you were born, just over the edge of your century, in a
small town in hesse, that the RAF put on the map by
obliterating it. i remember the photo of your parents on
the bookcase, just above the never-opened memoirs of
kropotkin, just below the hanging star of david and the
line drawing of herzl. your father was an autocratic
cantor who looked like lenin. your mother was martha
washington in a wig, virginal begetter of a dozen
children. i never met your parents. their bones are in
the soil of germany.

you stole coal from the freight yard as a boy, went
touring french youth hostels, were terrified by
masturbation. were enlisted with your siblings to tear
toilet paper every friday so as not to sully the sabbath
with menial labour. you smoked on shabbas once, and
one of the catholic boys told your father in order to
provoke him into beating the shit out of you, which he
obligingly did. you went to america on your way to
palestine, stopped there the rest of your life, what with
anti-semitism and impending bad times couldn't get a
job as a diesel engineer, got rich designing store fronts
and making gismos during the war, commanded the
loyalty of your workers and your boy scout troop,
cultivated constipation and migraine, held my mother
in check, tormented me and laid the foundations of
ecstatic despair.

you bit the bullet all your life and the dust in 1979.
i'd left you thirty years before, but you didn't go until
today. unlocking myself, i set your spirit free. you may
roam with the wind now, carrying my forgiveness and
almost love.
bye bye, dad. bye. take care. bon voyage.

111

krishna's soliloquy

(variations on a theme from the bhagvad-gita)

it's all right, arjuna. remember though you pull the
bowstring and release the arrow, it is i, not you, who
kill them and i have done so already. it is i who have
dreamed the cannon which will thunder after you are
dead and mythologized, arjuna, & my dreams, being
the hallucinations of vishnu, must come to pass.
likewise, the keeping of the wardrobe is my dream, &
long after your royal raiment has gone to dust, cohorts
of queens will wear uniforms of death, swords of
execution and medals which mimic the stars, to their
weddings, to herald the coming conception of future
princes. great musicians will celebrate the hunt and
the war, and blood shall be smeared across the pages
of many epic poems. i have dreamed cadavers of
genocide and it will come to pass. one day, arjuna, i
will teach your dead relatives to crack the presumed
illusion of existence at the seam, releasing the power
of stars and sun. my dream, distorted and perverted
through the broken prism of their history, will
proliferate these minuscule suns which they will aim
at each other's throats. then they will remember the
once greenness of this valley we ride through, you as
passenger, i as charioteer. they will begin to defuse a
very few of their stars of destruction, while seeking
ways to assemble others out of the fragments of
dismantled weapons and broken promises. they will
call this peace. they will celebrate. two rulers, more
mighty than kings, will shake hands. and as they part,
to tend their respective empires, one will salute the
other, in the name of this new-found peace.
with the roar of cannons.

<u>silkscreen on air</u>

can you break time and live? can the depression that
follows the soaring sleigh ride above the peaks of the
outer reaches of imagination yield to years of
transcendence of the tawdry evisceration of one's
native century. news items and cultural mandates
shoot the flyer down from the place where the
permanent injustice of existence is interwoven with
the intrinsic ecstasy of that very same beingness. can
the elegance of the song save? can love laughter
tears rage embroider the page of the illuminated
manuscript of the invisible book? can you look and
not become salt? can you enter minerva's womb and
<u>stay</u> there, compassionate and free, yourself the
symphony, the unpolluted river, the mountain, the
voracious sea of perpetual now and always here,
even beyond being itself, in shattered space ...
forever minus a day?

<u>bus ride in wales</u>

riding on the bus, crossing the river teifi,
i look out of the window and i say "that's me:
i am the waterfall; i am its turbulence; i am
its joyful sorrow; i am the quietude lurking
beneath the white water; i am the tension in
its molecules, the electricity in its atoms,
the explosions in the branches of the trees
above it, waiting through winter to wake into
leaf, elegant in their naked potentiality;
i am the dirty window of the bus, blurring
the view; i am the bus rattling through its
cosmos from there to here; i am the bus driver
and the passengers and everything that ever
was or will be."

non-euclidian variation on a phrase by jacob bush

who with this engine with its rattling bones

comes tearing down the beach and scattering stones

& poorly taking corners of the soul

in high winds of the mind, in swirling sands

that cover lines between the various lands

where naked & half broken, this very engine stands

or swerves & splutters, quite beyond control -

who with this engine, dying, torn with pain

still makes music gods cannot explain

beyond this time, this place, this grim terrain

that makes ten thousand shattered atoms whole

who with this engine randomly created

or with care evolved but desecrated

sanctified & lacerated

with this engine liberated

mining sunbeams, rainbows, emeralds, tin & coal

who ... with ... this ... engine ...

on being

(for my mother)

this is a bird
the outline of the shadow of whose wings on my heart
may be lost if i do not swiftly
record its song

was it herodotus then who said
that the same foot does not step
in the same stream twice?

this is the bird of my definition

i am not who i was a moment ago
nor who i will be a moment from now

i am all but none -
my most compelling words are couched in silence

was it dylan thomas then who spent all morning
removing commas
and all afternoon putting them back?

was it whitman who never stopped writing?
mother teresa who never stopped loving?
prometheus who never stopped rebelling?

the instamatic photograph ...
fades before it is taken

<u>the root of the difficulty</u>

the root of the difficulty is in the marrow of the universe

the root of the difficulty is in the very possibility

       of anything existing

the root of the difficulty is in the abstract disembodied

       mathematics of possibility

the root of the difficulty is <u>meta</u>mathematical

       the shadow that requires no light

       cast by the dream

       that requires no dreamer

the root of the difficulty is beyond time

the root of the difficulty has no beginning

the root of the difficulty is all that there is

it is the sculptural tragedy

the anguished ecstasy

the non-ending hyper-iterated trans-dimensional

       supra-infinite teleology of

       dancing shiva's flashing

       crown of thorns

preface

my body is badly bruised
my soul is wounded
and yet i have bent space
and broken time
and fly, angry and elegant
blue, with teeth chattering
among angels of conjured dimensions
who, pure among the stars,
wing banners of mystical tongues
and sing ... the internationale

<u>one life in the day</u>

fear, madness & birth at 2 in the morning

pass a bicycle pump at the bottom of the stairs and see

the black rabbit of death

drink peppermint tea in bed at dawn

look at a glass of water at an oblique angle

and see the rainbow

having found the ultimate joy, eat yoghurt & honey

as someone comes to you

and asks you what's wrong

open your mouth to sing

and only a bird flies out

just a few friendly words

they were impaled upon friendly bayonets

they were killed by friendly fire

they were crushed beneath friendly tanks

they were incinerated by friendly napalm

they were pulverized by friendly bombs

they were bullshitted by friendly communiqués

nothing like the camaraderie ... of battle

self-portrait

i am in the hills with che. the rifles are stacked.
the peasants will not revolt. when they revolt they
will revolt against me. when they topple the barons,
it is i, the premature revolutionary, who will be the
first to go to the guillotine, my head will converse
with those of the queen, the baptist and holofernes,
towering pygmies from the rain forests of memory
have sawed off the barrels of rifles and turned
them into flutes with which to converse about
epistemology with territorial birds. i am in the
hills alone. god ... he, she, it, they, me, you,
whatever ... has permitted the caves to open,
messiahs to rise, dragons to roar, incinerators to
burn, gas chambers to exterminate, screams to persist,
sorrow to flourish and flower in every stream. i am
in the hills, masterless, guruless, lost, found,
unbeholden to another's dream, i _am_ the stream,
dried, choked, flowing, angry, tranquil, interdependent,
independent. i am rain. it is no use
for you to read these words; you must find your own.
i am in the hills where abraham and che sleep in
mutual death. it is the beginning. the air rustles
imperceptibly. a single blade of grass is being born.

of bird and man

i used to imagine i knew what birds said.
long time ago in new york i fancied that birds
envied me being free to walk on the ground
and not having to fly and going into buildings
at night, opening my briefcase and letting
out the sun. i no longer have to imagine.
i've lived in the country so long now i
know what the birds are saying. there's
a certain special twitter after it rains.
that means, "hey kids, water!" i know
that cuz when i melt the ice block in
the garden so there's water in their pan,
they give off exactly the same twitter.
well, actually, bird talk isn't quite as
precise as all that. cuz today it wasn't
raining and their water wasn't frozen but
i went into the garden to round up some
garbage to throw away and the birds gave
that water call like maybe they were
saying "here's the dude makes our water
when it's cold." on the other hand, they
may be a good deal more sophisticated
than i'm giving them credit for. i'm
pretty sure i heard one of them say, "hey
this guy thinks he's got us all decoded
and he's gonna write one of those modern
poems about us." i heard another one say
"let's do a traditional one about him."
"ok," sez bird number three, "here goes ...
'hail to thee blithe scrivener ......
shelley thou never wert'"

<u>circle dance</u>

it's not what we believe
or what we say we know is so
it's the indissoluble mystery
that makes the dancing spirit glow

be it electrons or be it elves
that dance around the rim of the atom
it doesn't really matter a damn
or signify a datum

it's what we feel when we are real
it's what we paint when we don't paint
it's what we sing when we don't sing
it's what we rhyme when we don't rhyme
the bell that needs no ringer
the chronometer out of time

it's not what we believe
or we're so sure we know is so
but the indissoluble mystery
that makes the dancing spirit glow

<u>an explorer's soliloquy</u>

i'd gone a long way, and i retraced my steps a lot too, just
to make sure i was on the right track. they couldn't have
wanted me to start the journey because there were these bars
in the stone down where the water sporadically went, so i
persevered, followed the tubular passages, stopping now and then
to lick some nourishing limescale off one or other of my feet until
i came to an enormous slippery white valley just past
a circular grid and after i went exploring a bit, it began to look
like there was no way out except back the long schlep where
i'd come from and i wasn't going to do all of THAT.
one time when i was making my yumptieth attempt to get out
of the slippery valley, some big creature comes along and
makes these weird sounds like "come on arachne, baby, i'm
going to give you a hand." and this big white piece of flat
paper comes plopping down in front of me. i guess the
creature expected me to walk on it. well i might have been
a half-orphan, protein, after all, being in short supply. but
my <u>mother</u> taught me a thing or two. so i turned around and what
do you think? the piece of paper pursued me. well, i turned
around again. i'm going to find my <u>own</u> way. would YOU trust a
hand coming out of the sky?

scrimshaw

my reindeer and i were running late in our journey
from lapland to scotland. so i booked two rooms
in an english hotel and after stopping off briefly in
the bar, we got onto the lift. no-one had objected to
my reindeer when I was knocking down my whiskey
but now the hotel manager ran onto the elevator and
said, "sir, you cannot take your goat to your room."
i explained that (a) this was not a goat but a reindeer
and (b) he had his own room, thank you very much.
he said sorry but wild animals were not allowed in
hotel rooms, even their own. I explained that the
reindeer was not wild, which his gentle demeanor
in any case proved, but the hotel manager would not listen
to reason and we had to continue on our way. fortunately,
the reindeer hadn't had anything to drink,
so he was able to do the driving.

on the manufacture of rubies

oh, that ruby -
well, i'll tell you where it came from:
i just projected outward
a single drop of blood within me
which rang, which sang
which danced as if it had reason to

oh, that dancing drop of blood -
well, i'll tell you where it came from:
remember that rainbow you excitedly
showed me maybe five or six
centuries ago?
the taste of that rainbow
fell into my file cabinet and
i was cleaning out my file cabinet today
and the taste of that rainbow leapt out
and started to play the violin

oh, that rainbow, whose taste upon maturing
could play the violin -
don't you remember where it came from?
it came from the wild, mad, unreasonable
anticipation of a single musically inclined
drop of blood - the kind that begets rubies.

impressions of diaghilev's foot

diaghilev told stravinsky off
about pulcinella -
the music - i think he said -
was not quite 18th century enough
for the theme

as for the sketches
he'd commissioned from picasso -
diaghilev hit the ceiling ...
these were definitely not
what he'd had in mind

he threw picasso's sketches
on the floor and stomped
on them

how much am i bid
for this picasso
which bears the imprint
of diaghilev's foot?

<u>a cautionary nightmare scenario for
the 200th promenade concerts, 2095</u>

"accuracy is not the truth"
- henri matisse

to recreate the authentic atmosphere

already recreated at the 100th promenades

we will again use gut strings

for that authentic swing

but this time perhaps the guts

of those neo-castrati

who, owing to shortages of costly

medicines and care,

perished in the operation ...

<u>only</u> castrati may sing in the hunting songs

the battle hymns

the requiem mass -

old fashioned 20th century sampling techniques

will be used to overdub

the screams emanating from

our modern death row ...

flags will wave and dinosaurs be excluded

as no effort is precluded ...

for progress in authenticity

nineteen-fifties incident
(an allegorical tale)

mister metaphor

arrived at the doctor's

east eighties professional apartment

in new york city,

staggered to the couch

fell upon it and expired -

analysed to death ...

it was as if fate

had not similied upon him

why you should ignore this poem

am i the me that i was

when i said other than now i say?

which of yesterday's poems am i?

am i the intolerance that i was

for eyes i have since learned

to see through?

how many perspectives can dance

in one history?

am i now the solution

of no solution?

am i the me that i will be?

is that old man the young boy

some of whose memories he includes?

who was that young boy

of a thousand disparate potentials?

here - don't take what i said

yesterday for granted.

or even today.

or tomorrow.

unpunctuated

has the world ever been more
convulsed than it is right now
the cottages still sleeping while
my biro scratches the page
and my heart beats with
the thump of marching feet
right now this moment being
all moments all places all people
all revolutionary times revanchist
movements all bewildered poets
clerics trade unionists barricade
builders passive resisters storm
troopers hysterical ranters
lovers haters flower growers
people my brothers in fields
of pennsylvania missouri
virginia digging bayonets into
each others bowels my sisters
sewing bandages and stars
onto differing flags my cousins
on reservations and in camps
of detainment relocation concentration

forests felled for millions

of crucifixions thoughts passions

dreams burned at stake john

brown and his men hung for treason

mckinley invented tyranny in stone

assassinated transmuted into a

mountain and scaled welsh fusiliers

displaced sons of coughing displaced

miners wandering lost in bosnia

africa rising the tides changing and

changing and changing faster than we

can ever name them my brothers my

sisters my comrades my enemies i

love you listen listen listen listen

in your heart is a dungeon and

in that dungeon rosa luxemburg

still lives and sings

brief history-cum-petitionary prayer

it used to be cleaner
they'd tie your hands behind your back
with thongs or braided grasses
and spear you up to the hungry maw
of the carnivorous volcano
and throw you in to propitiate
the gods that could keep
the volcano sleeping
or the rains and crops coming
or victory for the chosen tribe to be assured

it used to be cleaner
the countess bathing
in the blood of a thousand virgins
to guarantee her continued youth
desirability immortality

now scientists diddle with superworms
who can live five times as long
this having obvious human implications
and unaffordable prolonged superannuations
are prevented by charging
for the gift of commencing
or continuing life

we can't afford
this paradise we've created
with its exquisite sunsets
colored by pollutants
with cough of asbestos coal
or whatever exported to
wherever hunger might breed
the greatest gratitude

our weapons are too expensive
to allow treatment for the ills they create
our chieftains of industry
information and the press
too hungry
their whores and gods too avaricious

we still engage in human sacrifice
perhaps we'll get as honest
about it in sufficient time
as our ancestors were
if so
the gods willing
perhaps there's a chance we might stop

<u>fiction is</u>

fiction is incompletely perceived reality
a drama enacted in one or two scenes
a battle of wills between differing
strains of larva on a single leaf
commercial exploitation of colliding planets
memoirs of ministers and presidents
jazzmen rockers coal miners prostitutes
robbers robin hoods and angels with
butterfly wings symbolic statements
abstractions encapsulated philosophies
non-objective car chases in free verse
holy or tawdry love songs in metered rhyme
guile disguising sincerity
the earth rising to a lover's touch
a broken typewriter's despair
torches and scorches and sunsets and rain
the lonely sigh of a subatomic particle
the vast stretches of horizons beyond existence
fiction is completely perceived reality

fate is

fate is a peculiar engineer

fate is the vector analysis of the soul

unchosen, it chooses

what one wins and

what one loses

and what we gain retain and lose

as an aggregate of the whole - -

some are born with

silver death warrants in their mouths

some with clouds & sky in their eyes

some with grey highways

that swerve like dreams

past tribal ruins

where the latest hypothesis dies

fate packs the universe in a trunk

fate is drunk, fate is brave

fate paves the heavens with lightning

concertos thunder and bird chirp

is costly inexpensive dear

fate is a peculiar

engineer

is is

is is a projection of my perception
as armies and peace marchers
contend in the non-euclidian plane
of my brain
a very partial resolution
of inputs outputs sideputs
regressions cycles revolution
is is is not
is not is is
is is neither how nor what
is may even be deception
is is the perception
of your careening
involuntary projection

<u>fantasy is</u>

fantasy is speckled speculation
heavy light as it crushed the candle
or falls with a plop
from the headlight in the fog
fantasy is a chicken's revenge
as it reads the entrails
of a battery of men
transmutation of die-hard rabid myths
into gothic vampires and heroic playboys
the alchemy of death itself into
wicked cadavers, turin shrouds,
delicate wings that sing of life and legacy
fantasy is misguided, guided,
opportunist, revealing, liberating
by turns ...
fantasy heals the wounds it creates
and dresses fantasy's burns
fantasy is ten thousand cinematic succubi
dancing through the dreaming head of a teenage boy
caruso, elvis, oasis, blur
rattling in the ears of a girl
the speck of imagination that sometimes
in some strange way comes true
or forever rings false
the mendicant mirthmaker
who laughs at astronauts
where the medieval angel vaults

question is

is a door a duncan dances through
is a doubter tapping his fingers
a hitch-hiker thumbing a lift
on the heavy vehicle of enquiry
a jazzman in a smoky club
urging his sax into shattering inflection
bessie smith shrugging her shoulders
then pointing in any direction
question is what is why is
what on earth the sky is
if i decide to be born
what will my pay be
is you is or is you ain't
my maybe

<u>fibonacci is</u>

is

well

a very

strange sequence of

numbers or in this case

words that at least in theory could continue

in that way mimicking growth and possibility

         and music painting and such forever

a dream is

a dream is an esoteric guide
   to the numbers racket
a dream is a straitjacket
   for sigmund freud
a dream is joseph's ticket
a dream is an opportunity
   for a poet to plagiarize himself
a dream is an undecipherable
   and impenetrable code
a shredded recollection of
   tomorrow
a technicolor song of the open road
stravinsky's inspiration
st john's sorrow
the appearance of a molecular
   diagram in sleep
a dream after all is only a dream
for a child who begs whoever
   her soul to keep
like anything else
a dream is never what it seems

<u>serenade to a mealy bug</u>

the mealy bug proceeds determinedly
in straight line trajectory across
the dusty mustard colored nap
of the synthetic plateau that is
my bathroom floor rather quickly
for a creature of this size
as if it knows exactly where it is
going and why, arrives at the base
of a dark brown polysomething
bucket beneath my sink, which it
circumnavigates until it disappears
from view leaving only its memory
behind. i try to reflect on it
in its own terms and of course
i can't. for starters, as far as
i know it has no vocabulary.
it is unaware of nuclear radiation
which could exterminate my species
with imponderable consequences
for its own, yet seems to have
no need of euclid to apprise it
of the rudiments of first level

plane geometry. and then i realise
what the mealy bug and i have in
common aside from the raw fundamental
of life itself. a goal - in a
given direction - but subject to
circular diversions ... defined
i suppose in the limited topography
of this species or that but really
just boiling down to a kind of
pushing more deliberate than that
of grass or weeds, more demure than
that of wild horses, but as much a
mystery to me as it is to the
mealy bug.

<u>there is no poem</u>

there is no poem
there is the cracking tension
      in my bones as the
      pitiful beast riddled
      with remorse tries to crack
      out of the confines of myself
      and clutch at imagined blue tails
      of exuberant supernovae
there is no poem
there is the screeching as in
      ungraphited unlubricated
      undulations between acceptance
      and rebellion against my very
      self for having the audacity
      to take nourishment while
      billions starve
there is no poem
      there is the pyrotechnic anguish
      at every injustice that i am
      inexorably drafted in to
      be part of even as i oppose
      and there is the jade stream
      and the grasshopper and
      the winter ice and the
      brace of bluetits pecking
      at the peanut bag hanging
      outside the kitchen window
there are dreams, ecstasies, misgivings,
      surprises, screams, compassions,
      the shuffle of dancing feet, the
      migrating geese, sorrow and
      laughter and tears and release
      but no, never in the entire
      universe
is there a poem

on the manufacture of emeralds

suppose we define god

as the twitch inherent in supposing -

in that case there is god

big bangs here & there

imply respites erupting

into palpable beinghood -

these become universes

incredibly interesting things happen

in these universes

including the evolution of creatures

capable of shutting it all out

and creating boredom

on the other hand, a few evolve -

women, children, poets,

                philosophers, cats

capable still

of perceiving the excitement

in a drop of water

these two types of intelligence

provide shadow and light

for each other

moonbeams nestle passionately

beneath the leaves of the boredom tree

from such collisions, music evolves -

when control and release dance

elegantly together

the music itself can paint pictures

the pictures can sculpt

and the only failures that matter

are those with nerve endings

in this context,

god combs her long starry hair

and all the universes and eternities

are her way /// of contemplating herself

on the manufacture of diamonds

i ask myself what i am doing

wandering among pyramids & exotic shapes

architectural mounds of primordial memory

wandering through the winding souk

to the zocco where acrobats invoke deities

and magicians ply their trade - - -

myself being a rabbit

and all the magicians being otherwise engaged

i pull myself out of a hat

moménto lírico

no, one broke through and flew
to some chimney pot somewhere

he had thought
that all the blackbirds were
hiding behind the solid slate sky –
he wondered idly whether
the slate quarry was still operative

not that long ago the telephone
had roused him from a sunlit sleep –
echoes in his eyelids of only yesterday

there had been that boy behind the window
twelve perhaps
maybe thirteen
bliss on his face
power in his legs
as he bicycled into the wind that even now
magically quivers the twiglets on the bush

something's not falling apart –
the old man's bones are cracking
his gut is as riven and he thinks of dylan thomas
"the unicorn evils run him through"
his
pajama bottoms are falling down,
the wall repels pictures put there long ago
to create an atmosphere –
he prittsticks reinforcements and tries to remember
emerson lake and palmer's version
of moussorgsky's pictures from an exhibition,
safety pins his pajamas
but something is not falling apart

he remembers the wind of a few days ago
whistling like a boy through the letter slot
moaning like a diva
wailing like janis joplin

his memory stretches
like the elastic of his pajamas
and he is the boy

over a wind tossed ocean
whereon once he unraveled
the winding sheet of magellan

bicycling madly
past tree
past marine park and floyd bennet field
over the metal grating of the bridge
to the riis park shoreline
and along the shore
over the brooklyn boundary
all the way to far rockaway in queens
where he stands breathless and watches waves
taller than houses
make love to the sandy shore

back again
past his house and all the way
to the quiet lake in prospect park

water is water whether ocean
lake
or slate sky hiding blackbirds

something is mended
it'll come apart again
but it'll keep being mended

the old man looks at his welsh valley
scans the hills

no longer able to pick the rubbish off the lawn
he puts his hand over that part of the vision

but even litter is the world
in his mind he kicks candy wrappers on a flatbush street
he's holding his grandmother's hand and
        wearing a "green nose" that fell from a tree

it's one world after all
one time

he hums, sings in a broken whisper
"gimme the moon over brooklyn"
and
"blackbird singing in the dead of night,
take these broken wings and learn to fly"

he remembers passionate ocean breaking on pacific shore
on atlantic freighter
on cornish coastline
in welsh estuary

the old man is on a satellite

going round and round
        and round and round

<u>transparency</u>

look at the window pane
Read it (!)
watch the raindrops like tears
being pulled toward the center of the earth

watch that maverick raindrop there
deflected by what unperceivable
speck of airborne injustice
veer at a right angle
as lacking in verisimilitude
as truth itself
before finding precisely that part of the glass
on which to continue its journey

(conjunction of fate and free will?)

listen to the whistling howling shrieking wind
take on board its politics
find peace in the eye of the storm

look at the window pane
tell me everything you see

tale from a parallel universe

coleridge dismissed kubla khan as a mere fragment
and fed it to his personal shredder, stuffed the
results into the guinea pig cage where the beasts
burrowed in it and did what guinea pigs do. the
only copy of the ancient mariner got lost on the
way to the photocopier place and somehow wound up
as wrappings for the fish and chip shop.
coleridge's catalogue of his laundry however was
discovered by a diligent scholar and formed the
basis for a doctoral dissertation on early english
list poetry. and so it goes.

portrait of the crocodile

the crocodile loves her children
the crocodile feeds her children
    poets and boat repairpeople
    and the odd opera singer
it is not the crocodile's fault
    that cold-blooded is a symbol of
    whatever it may be a symbol of
    among a species famous for
    gratuitous slaughter
the crocodile
    having become a multipurpose
    metaphor
    lives in the past and
    addresses you with language
    she herself does not speak
the crocodile is
    a freelance demographer
the crocodile never
    has to get this morning's news
    into perspective

<u>winding the springless clock of recall</u>

the streets of those dreams are like merging memory
which is to say the splayed chicken innards
of divination which is to say a
history that plays tricks with time,
fablizes the should have been obvious,
narrow randomly intersecting streets of
balkan kismet in old new york,
the bone marrow, the skeleton key,
the circle dance of the circle line,
italio-hispanic swahili yoruba celtic
mohawk judaic cantonese korean vietnamese
german cajun russo-ukranian scandinavian et cetera
blues purple against the catacomb sky.
no broad boulevards,
the only red squares interspersed with black,
washington square knights move
leaving henry james behind
as falla anoints a tree with meaning
and visiting housewives discus
flying saucers left over from tupperware parties.
grandma's roadmapped translucent wings
swoop and buzz the scene serene
with cappuccino hendrix at wha,
slick airplane hangared at go-go,
disappearing books on eighth,
mathematico-poetic dragonettes in shoestores,
reverberations of both dylans,
in coalescence of carefully ordered
chaos of the streets of those dreams.

1918

grandfather was twice over in love or something like that.
in any case he was young, and barely explicable juices that
dominated his spirit and infiltrated his soul were not to be
contained by imaginot things like siegfried lines dug with blood
into dispassionate earth nor the gunpowder scented rain that
watered the friendly anemones he brought in his spiked helmet to
chez mademoiselle. the news of his twice over love travelled
quicker than anyone might have preferred as allied bombs (as if
bombs had identities or allegiances) exploded in the park across
the road from the house in frankfurt where grandmother, not that
many years after weaning mother's kid brother, kept migraine at
bay at the end of a needle with medically sanctioned morphine.
grandfather arrived home, torn in two by war and defeat, and
grandmother battered by perceptions that twice infinity equalled
zero, soldiered on with him. years later, grandmother and
grandfather lay buried side by side, blamed for everything, for
having sanctioned the digging of the wrong ores at the wrong
times in the wrong places by the wrong methods and for the
wrong reasons, while somewhere in france perhaps some fresh
anemones lay at an anonymous grave, wrapped in the anomalies
of the morning news.

hill resident, global village

zarovski lives in a mindfield

where scuffled dried brooks

residues of proud ancient rivers

run through undefinitive mountains

reduced to hills by cadences of sand and stone

marking uncertain boundaries

between ancient bloodthirsty empires.

the ironed horse runs on time and water

waits for no one

stomps on refrigerator cartons

crushes old fashioned portable typewriters

will trade you a kalashnikov for twenty camels

fashioned of virginia tobacco

it is certainly not the role of the poet

it is not the role of the poet
to explain the world to itself

it is not the role of the poet
to explain
or deify
the incomprehensible

it is not the role of the poet
to untangle the thread of existence
to weave or recreate
carnivorous mythologies

it is not the role of the poet to blame
to berate
to dress justice in the robes of retribution

it is not the role of the poet to hunt
or to hunt hunters

or to forgive
and in so doing put the poet higher
or to get rich
or to worry about
immortality
or about mortality

or to wear chains
or to beat the poet or others with branches
or with clever words

or to write poems
or to make lists
or to enter lists
or to suggest for one moment
that the poet exists

it is not the role of the poet
to demand the formality
of informality

or to try to stop
language

or to stop abstracting
whatever image or images
begin to emerge

reflections on reflections

suppose what i see
when i watch my hand writing
as that's my outside
then that's my image
when i look into the mirror
that hangs on the bathroom wall
what i see is not my image
but a reflection of my image

then i pick up a hand mirror
and hold it behind my head
at an appropriate angle
to see the back of my head
well, not the back of my head
but the reflection in the wall mirror
of the reflection of the hand mirror
of the image of the back of my head

tilting the hand mirror a bit
i see a distant reflection
of my own eyes peering
my own smile worn thin
through a series of reflections
as well as my less distant reflection
looking bemusedly on

i go to the front window
look out at an apricolored street light
in the misty purple-blue darkness
close one eye for clarity
then close the good eye
and look out through
a ripe but inoperable cataract
and see a ring of lights instead

like fairy lights or
ezekiel's flying saucer
hovering over
projected perplexity

how many angels does it take
one wonders
to dance on the head
of the pushpin on the
bulletin board
housing the cobwebs of
parallaxed memory
how much kandinskied kandifloss

how many governments does it take
to make one anarchist
how many wars to make
one pacifist
how many socialisms blow in the wind

i carry these thoughts around
tilt with radios, typewriters
tape recorders, pens,
watch my hand on the pen
as i write these words
and mouth these sounds

what is it i hear
and what do i see

<u>introduction to classical philosophy</u>

having been waylaid by a daffodil
and intercepted by a book
on the way to the picket line

no it wasn't exactly that way ...
there was this book
by lucretius
translated into modern english
as
on the nature of things or something like that

it had a lovely cover
green dustjacket
big yellow writing

looked grand on my
laboriously painted
vermilion bookcase

after painting the bookcase, i rested
then i got a job
in a paint warehouse

i never did read the book
but the cover was a knockout

education's grand y'know

actually the only difference between
        a writer and other people ...

is a writer sometimes writes

who i am

i was born with at least
    two identities
one napoleonic
    from left to right
one judaic
    from right to left

there was little overt
    correlation between them

i, or whatever
    vector resolution i signify
by stages
    evolved or synthesised a
self-semi-consistent identity

these few lines have germinated for years
concentrated for days
sublimated for hours

constitute my

left-handed compliment
or complement

) to myself (

<u>yarn</u>

the cat moves tentatively –
is this ball of yarn alive (?)

the cat is white and ginger
its motions monochrome and careful –
the ball of knitting wool
the always color of mystery

perhaps the cat is trying
to unravel
the yarn

the cat is almost nonverbal
and so a creature of mystery too
like the disembodied material itself

the cat wonders in its nonverbal way
is this something to eat
to guard against
to enquire into
to understand

the cat walks in front of a hospital

encounters an old man with a

sheaf of A4 papers and a fineline pen

the cat says "meow"

the old man says

"sorry, cat –

i would stroke your head

but i've hurt my back

and besides

you might have fleas

and they might

set off the mobile phones

before i have time to

roll my already partly tangled

skein of thoughts and perceptions

into some kind of coherent

preliminary draft of a

theory of epistemology"

cat's whisker

look at that
imagine imaginary cat
sitting on a tuft of imagination
swatting at a nameless butterfly
in no way perturbed
by the fact that it misses
so engrossed
that imaginary cat in my imagination
misses the speculative horizon by a

<u>atmosphere</u>

this "breaking of the waters"
   - is it a term that
    midwives use or
    weather forecasters
    or biblical prophets

a work of art being a talisman
a poem or whatever being a work of art
      made of sounds and symbols for sounds

the poem being a tallis
    when the dew is deep on the hill
both beckoning and avoiding understanding
like some revolutionary monk
looking at the sky's extraordinary bangles

sensing yet another
    undefined revolution

taking care not to whisper too loudly

while stealthily stealing raindrops

<u>concerning the dust mite</u>

the most powerful household creature
        is the dust mite
no may bees about it
        it is faster than
        any vacuum

there is no point in trying
        to scare the shit out
        of the dust mite

it hides deep in the nap
        of the carpet
defecates up to eight times
        its own weight
        per news broadcast
is as tenacious
        as say, diogenes

it feeds on dandruff
        and shredded words
does not penetrate
        dōgen's dewdrop
or question marx

the shadow of the dust mite
leafs through intractable memories
of echoes of transliterated translations
        of tolstoy and turgeniev

the light of the shadow's echo
        illumines
                every
                    infinity

<u>a very slow letter to taurus the bull</u>

(written on st. david's day)

actually this is only concerning
the letter

first the matter of the
half-intended recipient

you know how constellations
are made

someone goes out at night
or into an observatory
or round the latest clock planetaria

and connects up dots
to make pretty pictures
of self-fulfilling prophesy

says aha, here is taurus the bull
zodiacal little rascal

some time passes
few thousand years or so maybe

and someone sends a pioneer called ten
possible only some time since
the revolutionary discovery
and positioning of nought

sends ten out through pretty rugged terrain
asteroid belts for instance
even more chaotic
than computerized bureaucracy
then past pluto
past persephone
who the media touted and then forgot

well past to where all that
localized debris becomes
well not exactly irrelevant
but somehow from a slightly
different neighborhood

not way out beyond the
spiral arm and all that
but far enough

to take whatever messages and regards
threats and kisses
guano from vampire bats
romantic vanilla from tathagata
switchblades by moonlight
flowers by dawn

will survive or accrue during the journey –
estimated delivery time
assuming it gets there
and stranger things happen
is meant to be 2,000,000 years

to a wonderous world where
perhaps no one starves
to a magical place
where trains never run late
for how can a train run late
when there is no train

to in short
a place of unimaginable efficiency
whose sorting office, if such there be
could well return the communiqué
to sender for clarification

meanwhile somewhere in
somebody's memory
an accidentally plucking rubber band
conjures childhood upon childhood
of empty wooden box guitars

imaginings way way way
out of the ballpark
way way way out past the outfield
past incomprehensible quantum
batting averages

to some conjured on an easel
constellation of digits and dots
and that's no bull

handle with care

this is my only possession now
handle it with care
the color of milky coffee
one seed, sunflowerseedlike -
it turned up during an otherwise
petit bourgeois dream
when a previously undisturbed
crevice of my brain
inadvertently got dusted -
i blame special effects
they do most of the dusting around here
and my job is creating dust
for special effects to deal with

there was a wild wind in my dream
so crevices are the only places a seed is safe
it was election day later this year
the wind tried to lift the sail like an awning
that i and some greysuited fellow were trying to hold down
he said it thought it was a ship at sea

the purpose of crevices you see
is to maximise surface area
thereby providing room
to store as much garbage as possible
to allow for inspiration
and egress
in the guise of the brain thereby imitating life
an accordion
or the mask of a concertina

soothing music for the
perpetually around-the-corner
economic collapse

before the wild wind in the dream
there was a news stand -
it was run by a middle-aged lady
called mary worth who used to appear
in one of the newspaper comic strips

she sold me a copy of life
and discussed the rosenberg case
with me

then came the election day storm

anyhow, i was telling you about this seed
it's tearshaped
sometimes special effects
gets the streamlining right

on some level it contains the
entire world -
it's all i've got

handle it with care

of protosaxophonic immanence

(for the lingering echo of john coltrane)

if i could be a saxophonist

if i could moan magnificently

thru the sunshine colored metal

conjuring heroic tragedy

from nearly silent turbulence

of remembered but viscerally

stochasticism - if i could be say

the metal itself of saxophone

the dark dungeon from

which is mined

the irrational lava

of molten apricot

if this could silence

the sinister clatter of sabers

this implicit universe

momently caged in dust

from which the lightning

hammers idea of saxophone

if i could echo that many universes

in this or that spontaneous string of moments

i would take note

<u>somewhat past the sand bar</u>
<u>between night and morning</u>

rain returned
its angle not visible from that room
turned underblanket up to 4
higher than that
    and steam would come
        out of my ears
drift back to sleep briefly
joe in bronx i think it was
recurrent
kafka's there
joe's in the habit
    of standing on his shoulders
also somerset maugham
these college kids he mutters
meaning me
i was 45 at the time
his classic i thought think
the one about the corrugated plant
abstracted into goodnaturedly doomladen
pre-euclidian parable
i'd worked there too
wondered why we hadn't
talked about the union
i get up and then wake
switch off the water heater
a new but other quirky
elemental morning begins

logomachy

words were suddenly rearranged
materialism idealism
had acquired meanings
that in our circle were discarded
it was mater-ism
and idea-ism
actually that we were
talking about –
conflicting linguistics
of disciplined liberation

we sat atop
mount comprehension
the most dangerous
volcano of all

when it's really raining nowadays
when my arthritis acts
up enough

that dynamic macro micro
cosmic interface
slides into oblivion

dark light, antimatter, are
shattered by raindrops torn
dripping incipient hurricane sleep

a wet lawn becomes a wet lawn
green foliage in grey light
blanketing lifetimes of rage

obeisance to an oblate spheroid

(for my extended family)

a deep blue vase
the deep blueness of its patina
infiltrating the earthenware
so that its imperfections
are perfections

except for the slight truncation
of the horizontal circular base
the bottom main body of the vase
is as spherical as anything real
could ever be

atop this is the long narrow
elegantly upright throat of the vase
dry since noah's sailing days.
belying the transcendent quenchingness
and purity of the water in the belly

that such a dream could occur
that such a dream could be joyful
on a chilly wet windy morning
that such blue could verge on purple
that jazz and poems meander

that pulsating illuminations
could pierce and shred for a time
all inevitable discontents
bespeaks that if there is anything at all
it is even more than everywhere

belated existential get-well-soon card to myself

welcome home but look
i'm not ready for ya

there i was tearing my microcosm apart
looking for just a few sheets of lined paper
whereby a fractured body
might properly welcome
a muse that suddenly fell silent
amidst the noise

generated by a fractured
already somewhat brittle femur

anyhow suddenly when i stopped
i found two pads of paper
so what was i worrying about -
the world hadn't ended yet

there's work to be done
crutches to brandish
universes to sing
scents and textures to describe
of all the lovely flowers and raindrops
and garbage trucks with jukebox lights
ecstatically singing
of gratuitous purgatory

<u>this is not the story</u>

this is not the story of lance
whose washing machine
malfunctioned in greenwich village
and who went on
to penetrate the skies of terra haute

it is not the story
revealed by revelatory dreams
nor exactly hinted at
by mars outside the front door
even before i could look
left of a blue star or planet
whose name but not whose music
escapes me

this is not even the story
of the author who at age 16
took a girl to a gene krupa concert
and as she was so beautiful
did not so much as kiss her
for fear that she would disappear
into mists of memory
that decades on
hint at something
that perception can at most sing about

this is not the story of the boy
who at 18 read stalin and descartes
because the dust jackets appealed to him
this is not the story of anything ...
it is however a knitted garment
made of the invisible fabrics
of striving of almostness
of conjecture

<u>early morning mood piece</u>

it is dark chilly wet
not exactly windy but
the air snaps

nothing visible in the sky
save foggily illuminated clouds

a vehicle across the road
has one of those bumps on the top
signifying SPECIAL MESSAGE

this large car or small bus
is for tours, bands, footballers
no is an ambulance or
something to do with police
or matters even more mysterious

i close the door again
hurry back to the kitchen
for an urgent call
on the conch shell
and a cup of peppermint tea

by definition

it wasn't a barn dance

it was mostly square dance

look out - the floor is made of glass -

it isn't but

knute rockney made a forward pass

and someone made a movie

there was a break for protest songs

the electricity of recognitions

friends acquaintances wives even

who would punctuate some of the years

it was magic actually

whether malenkov or mendeleyev

it was foreign

it was far away

it <u>had</u> to mean freedom

the yawning tortoise monologue

what shall i do
right now i'll scrawl my narrative
in the manner of tortoises
heckled through the millennia
for never overtaking achilles.

it is i after all who laid the
foundations for modern calculus
and all that followed it -
don't they know that
silly asymptotes?

achilles fired me
regarded me with disdain
sent me to the job centre with a note

"treat this creature kindly
it took a long time for it to reach you
even walking briskly for a tortoise"

my occupation really is
barndoor locker
but i'm always stuck
in a traffic jam

such a mob of metaphysicians
on the roads these days!

don't cry baby

don't cry baby
the porridge you spilt
is chock a block with stars
but mommy will mop it up
and hurl it into the dull damp sky

don't cry baby
the sky will not be illuminated
it will be our eyes
that shine like ornaments

don't cry baby
the dull damp sky
glowing in argon
like rancid marmalade
don't cry baby
daddy will mop it up

don't cry baby
celestial choirs
are singing your anthem
baby will mop it up

don't cry baby
baby will wipe
the telescopic mirror
and from the odd glimpse
here and there
build the sky anew

why i am generally cheerful

depression is an art
that requires technotantric
precision

i could never get the hang of it -
some kind of fury sometimes in sleep -
but hardly ever in the waking state

you get up in the morning
and schedule or rank
anticipated activities

it's early - only the owls -
(and i don't hear any)
are up before me

the dog next door is taciturn
carefully considering
the import of every bark

one day it will be cold enough again
for the bluetits to alight
on the peanut bag outside the window

confessions of a fortune teller

i was a soothsayer far to the east of here
it's all so blurred in memory
it was so many thousand years ago

my life hung on every line i wrote
and melodies of the sea
were blamed on me

i am the universal incomer
i wrap in words
things like scent and memory

i say nothing really
but i say it with passion and commitment

the job specifications have changed
the universe is going for a song

sixteen lines

of course every statistician

worth the salt statue

of the wife of lot

extrapolating into the horizons

is a diviner

lumbered with would and wouldn't

and we were doomed to lose

innocent fisherians cast adrift

in a tide of numbercrunching

bayesian monks

resurrected by

vanishingly small

computers

we slipped out into salt air

composed ourselves

and ran away from home

should symptoms persist

illness
is out of a mind of its own
peaks in peak periods
during holidays
when doctors are away
during unjust wars
there being no other kind
so that mars
falls into seas of
when history aches
when humanity itches
owing to stardust under its fingernails
owing to the blues of one blue planet
emerging from the coffee house
where mendelssohn and mingus
memorize elegant mutations
of old scores
and footballs footfall
teaming with life
pause, compose a thank you note
for the removal of thorns
take the tablets diligently
with plenty of water -
ride the coach of no reproach ...
travel inward then outward then inward again -
you're sorry
your wounds are scarry
the table leg is brittle
in need of some kind of splint or cast ...
that's the breaks

<u>floridian timescape</u>

conquista-centaurs with advisors
none the wiser
for their visor grilles
clipped the alligators
and arriving by sea
fondly lancing fronds
startled the humans
already present seeking past
all possible futures sought
eternal youth in the
heartland of swamps

centuries later it was
an election that was stolen
in that very subcontinent
that land of slaughter
and aspiration and
mythic fountains
trade union retirement homes
recollected cousins
recollecting ambiguities
rainbows bursting sadly madly gladly
sudden from sodden soil

only those of the words
lending themselves to transcription

i have within me
licorice whirlpools
chocolate waterfalls
unpaintable landscapes
undancable dances
silent ominous winds
rent skies of interior fires
merlin's unicycles
arthur's wheelchairs
despair hope humor pain
gorgeous purple fabrics
everything i've taught
learned forgotten confused
defied embraced
defined questioned
mathematecized dreamed
a love of humanity
that knows no bounds
or boundaries
save excruciating shyness
attendant to occupying a time
that contains you
that contains me
that contains all
that contains the foolish wisdom
of knowing unknowing everness

on the significance of frances

i asked her what does frances signify - she said it's a name - names don't signify - names are names - she was lying on her stomach, mopping great enormous swabs of grey dust with a great swabbing dustmop from under some elevated furniture in considerable haste - a guest is arriving she said - there is no time to waste - but i said i'm developing this character in my mind - i haven't written a short story for eons - long one for that matter - i need a frances - before you even take up pen and paper? she asked ... i'm a frances ... i'm a person not a name ... i mop ... i prepare for our guest ... i do not signify

i took up a red-earth colored blanket of great size and shook it out of the back door of the cottage. a little girl in a school uniform - eight maybe - blue tie - thin red stripe called out - "j - 10th letter of the roman alphabet - hello" and then walked in. frances said to her "you're chubby - you need to lose weight" - "not if i grow" the girl replied. shots rang out from nowhere. the three of us died. frances and the young guest ascended into the sky. wait for me i cried and jumped up off the roof of the house which grazing sheep entered. i never did find out what frances signified.

excuses excuses

poor wilhelmina
she ain't as free as they say
    it's been days now
    been dazed
since i saw her in luther's shop
sketched and drawn in her wheelchair
editing his theses
    i offered to take her out
    for a breath of fresh air
i wasn't myself
arguably i'm never myself
    i was ganesha-like
    except not elephant-headed
    as i'd never gotten
    to pack my trunk
but on some level
four armed is forewarned
    it was awkward
    getting my four sleeved coat on
    but luther helped
later hungry ravaged bears
snapped my dream shut
and i shook in teleological terror
    i reached for my hat
    held it over the edge of the bed
being in an experimental mood
i released it
    i was still on
    the planet i was born on
the hat fell to the floor

my hat did not need
an excuse to fall
    just an explanation
    which in rough terms
    was provided by gravity
    which
    when you come down to it
    is a word
and there in a word
or in any number of words
you have it
    i couldn't help
    falling in love
    any more than my hat
    could resist the gravity of analogy
look, alibis aside
i love you more than life itself
    i'll meet you on the picket line
try not to be late
    i'll be disarmed
    two-armed at most
you'll recognise me tho:
    i'll be the one
    carrying the placard
    that says
    "free will"

reflection looks back

to set his hobby horses out to graze
the old man opens but only momentarily
the front door to the rest of the universe

it is dark and chilly
with the chilliness of exteriorness
but the man looks up
confirming the continued existence
of the sky

the sky that is laden with gnats
delicate rainbows
and adverts for the terror
of nirvana

the old man

on the frailty of childhood and of legend

it was a while before
    they gave me a dictionary
i think the encyclopedia came first

how was it to occur to me
    to look up words in dictionaries
or to navigate by any but intuitive means

i didn't know what the hell
    a grail was and those
    arthurian legends carried me
    to where i didn't care

what mattered about the grail was
    that if lancelot found it
    whatever it was

guinevere would go to bed with him -
it was generally guarded
    by word-sculpted dragons

there were no bad guys in arthur
just enigmas

except for a later invention
called gawain supergood

he was a pain in the but

abstract condenser

(a pantheist perspective)

you know those times
   that you wrestle
      with the angel
      as if the angel
      actually existed

the outcome is   no outcome is possible
except you're gradually becoming
   an echo   a ripple
   a fading
   occasionally embellishing

memory

i'll lay 3 to 1 in favor of memory
   over chance any day

some of the times you sort
   of seem to win

it was the angel's patience
   that carried the day

the whole ball of wax being
an illuminating imaginative leap
in the thought processes
of a figment of your imagination

scene seen several decades later

the boy in the time machine
has a towel in his hand
the animation of discovery
the communication buzz

he stutters less than usual
as he dries dishes to the rhythm
of his mother's remarks about heine
his own about kramer

the rhythm of her washing slows
pacing itself to his drying
as the conversation veers
to the si gerson campaign

as the radio teeters
between beethoven and leadbelly
it must be the full moon
but it seems like yesterday

only it's today and she died just the other day
after things had slowed down
incredibly

on the distillation of water

i guess it was the angle
at which the rain beat against the wall
the particular wall it beat against
its infuriatingly undulating intensity
and the narrator trying to get some sleep

yes we live for the moment
but the moment was lasting for hours
not the requisite nanosecond
of an elusive transcendence
that rendered any such sound
at the far end of the house inaudible

i'd wake up with a start you see
- hooray it's quiet
my neighbors have turned their tap off
oh no no no
there it is mad mad mad
like some funky wet metronome

well face it this has happened often enough
there's the alarm clock which informs me
that if i want to reach tonight
in any kind of shape i'd better get up now

i abandon the sound to its own devices
and after minimal preparations
proceed downstairs – unlock the front door
to look out – it has been raining
the ground is wet
the sky is cloudy – i can't see a single star

but wait as i go to close the door
some wayward raindrop
clinging i think to a leaf
whispering to the leaf
in the language that raindrops speak
that raindrops and leaf
will be bonded forever

that raindrop catching the minimal
artificial light at some peculiar
and fleeting angle looks gemlike
undulating the orange hope
of the later sunshine
and the glittering pale blue promise
of a planet that dreamed it was a star

this is the kind
of three for a penny vision
that transforms people

a guy might possibly not recognise it
had he not been in greenwich village
about forty years ago
happy with his then
and vanished into memory
small czech chandelier
purchased from
a new jersey importer who had foolishly
engaged him as a statistician
before sensibly dismissing him

tilting his head then to coax the
hey hooray look at this –
revelatory colors out of said light
at the intersecting of some
didactic writing by huxley
and exuberant sedition by heim

that rattled around inside the narrator's head
and with other influences
pushed prodded accompanied him
through a diverse nonforseeable trajectory until he reached
a council house in rural wales where
almost a quarter of a century later he encounters
the messianic raindrop
on the leaf outside

now one day for sure
this narrator will be no more or less
than a memory
a memory who couldn't even make it
as a statistician for a lighting importer
and who therefore couldn't possibly know
whether or not at some future time
and unlikely as it may be
the speculation enters the whirling realms
of heuristic validation
a tourist bus might arrive
after a decent interval has passed

it is here that a mendicant poet
had discourse with a raindrop
that you need to travel your own
chaotic path to comprehend

<u>fashioned from readymade imagery,</u>
<u>a classical blues for passover chorus</u>

he was named after a musical instrument
& fled into the i – not the seeing
but the dubious identity of the needle

as if anyone thought that cleopatra
with her hieroglyphs & marc anthony
had it sewed up for all time

pursued by contemporary caesars
he impaled himself on the needle
and died - strange path for a son of song

as if messianic and in some way he was,
his father was not his father but
a gentle sorrowful gayness
in search of cover for its awayness

provided by his mother beaten into
caves of celebration by the out of step
more midnightness of her being

she provided wine for wedding guests
who in innocence she hurt
for she meant no harm
refugeeing down
elija's stars from city skies
ezekiel's wheel
from humanity's recurrent dreams

what i want for the 8th evening of chanuka

if anyone wishes to understand me –
if anyone considers it a worthwhile
    exercise to dig beneath what makes
    a faulted but generous hearted
    person like myself tick or twitch
    or write poems, compile errand lists
    ponder whether zero shouldn't
    logically be in the fibonacci
    sequence and then decide well
    of course it shouldn't be after all
    it is necessary to know what
    informs both the error and the
    virtue of my ways.
i am a pacifist and a pantheist
i am a commited socialist and an
    anarcho-syndicalist without knowing
    precisely how that would work
    or whether on some level it
    already does
i consider both a good blues song and
    a velikovskyite tract to be a kind
    of caress
i am a vegetarian
i am old
i am jewish
the reason i am not a traditional jew
    is that there are none
it's not an original idea that there is a
    judaic trinity but it is one i embrace
    with a passion that nearly wipes
    me out

there is of course aton from egypt
    adon adonolom adonoy light heat
    the sun, all suns – you can have
    too much of a good thing or too little –
    you can't lock the sun up in a
    tomb and moses and a bunch of
    other people walked to the red sea
    and it happened so long ago that
    there's no video of it but some say
    the sea parted
there is yahweh, jehova, wittgenstein
    the cracker of earths the
    irrational force to whom and or to which
    i illogically plead when it hurts enough
there is or are elohim the all pervasive
    the everywhere the me the you
    the imperishable mutating thru
    dreams and aspirations.
    that's the bit i really believe in
    – all the rest is only
    the ouch.

<u>from a windswept interior volcano</u>

if only zen masters
keep their cool
while opening plastic bags
there is something wrong
with industrial design

if only matter is abstracted
does meaning pre-exist the perceiver?

a tree in a forest…
that is the sound of one hand

it is morning coffee time
no more sleepy lagoon
mr poet

prospectus

well, y'see
      it creates employment

and it would be a waste
    of perfectly good manpower
    to inter living attendants
    to see to the needs
of our departed but not departed pharaoh

so one of the cleverer kids in the
    design department hit on this
    nifty idea of sculpting stone
    terra cotta whatever into an
    entire entourage for his
    mightiness

it saved lives   it created employment
and so long as we were nice to the
tomb of the emperor – our late king
having you know, an in with the sun, the
stars, the moon and other wonderous
things in the sky –

as long as we kept in good
with the monument that we had erected
there would be peace power prosperity
asteroids would hurl themselves
      at the earth
in obedient awe

i'm not gonna give this one a clever title

it's not the stories that i'm
    on about any more
i've learned to live with
    thousands of stories
that perpetually inhabit my soul

it's not that rare glimpse
    of something like that sunrise
    eleven or twelve minutes
    ago that people weather
    many years and disasters
    to see obscured by the
    sales pitches the chi squares
    glaring defiantly at
    the latest computer model

it's none of that

it's why one wrestles with the angel
whether the angel is there or not

look here, y'got the wrong guy
i'm a pantheist not an animist

this is the department of general
comprehension

particulars are over there
in the complaints department

on the one hand

lenin was a hero of visions
he'd travelled all the way
    from switzerland
to be with these mad
    georgian monks
and jewish intellectuals
    with high principles
    and elegantly convoluted dialectics

lenin proposed alliances
that would make the hair
on your elbows curl

he was in his bunker now
it was as if double track
and loops and all those
hyperbolics had already been invented

he picked up a red flag and
started dusting around the room
it was twin track like
you see he was dusting
the gifts of accident and whatever
two crystal balls contributed by
    sister parties in distant climes

enveloped by petrograds' chimes
getting a clear confused picture –
what d'ya call it
when there's two crystal balls

on the penetration of koans

peace has broken out

or in any case the potential

accordingly green tea sales are down

and economic collapse is never more

that a feather's flutter away...

in the trieste of the mind

in the novi vinodolski of memory

in the caverns of new york

songs rise up out of nowhere

and skate-boarding

monks assert

that it is the frictions

    between past and present

that cause the madness

    called the future

a few drops of water on the circular track

the circular track
is a particle accelerator
for high school students
which is to say
the students are the particles

it's a roulette wheel
but you've won
before you've started

it's a very orderly way
of going nowhere

the lovely thing about it
is you don't have to
get to the point

you can just go merrily
sadly reflectively along
making your own private
quantum leaps without some
aggressive gym teacher
yelling at you that there's
a train of thought to catch
or some psychiatrist
trying to interview
the rorschach sweat stains
punctuating your undershirt

it takes a few years -
you're seventeen now
and maybe by the time
you're seventy-five or so
you'll get some of it into perspective

the world will war and war
sadly that's what worlds do...
the world will love
with an awkwardness
that bespeaks redeeming features...
the world will wonder
will dance will hum
will walk on water

the world will scour the universe
looking behind every ear
every year, every star
for water to wring reason out of

what a lot of fuss
over a little burnt hydrogen

<u>identity</u>

i think i've discovered
    who i are
or maybe i should say
    we have
having been first introduced
    to the idea of i
when i was maybe
    nine years old ...
they had changed
    the grading system
    at school
it being in transition
    but we didn't know that then
from A to D to A to the
    dreaded F word
    whether that was freedom
    or failure or the letter
    after E for endurance
anyhow in that peculiar time
the new grading system went
    S I U - still inhabits
    that place in the cacophony
    i call my mind ...
    s for satisfactory   i for needs
    improvement   u for unsatisfactory
i inhabits the gray area
where life happens and shadows dance
i am you
all of you

deja shoe

myself when young did eagerly frequent
hiring halls and similar havens
of existential argument

once was hired by a shoe warehouse
lasted three weeks
you needed four weeks to be
a regular   to have seniority
to dwell on alphanumeric
shoe specifications
encapsulating
burying
the shoe's entire identity
as a size a gender a material
a time   an outline of itself
an inline of the rest of spacetime

so you'd think i could express
damn near anything
but i'm as stumped as the next person
on what words to use
to say what words cannot contain
after having been told
three times so far
this is our last serious
tenth planet of the sun
each time ignoring
their own earlier reports
by way of rebuttal

the third tenth planet name
the media have released
is alphanumeric
it seems that whether it fits or not
naming things is a contentious matter
and as in all insoluble
projective tests
the shoe must go on

i don't understand it either

there i was in the wake
translucent images
    leading graven by a hair
it was the first time
    the balance had
        tipped that way
my grandmother had just died
        and it was 1956
come to think of it grandpa
        had died in 1950
and a lot had been happening since then
but this was pivotal
    just before i'd seen scots
        and irishmen fighting in
        the street when i knew
        they weren't there
for highly suggestible types like me
    the news is pretty mixed these days
always was
next wraith i saw was my own
me
according to almost universal folklore
a guy sees his own wraith ...
that's three days before his death ...
that was many years ago
i never told anyone back then
i've never seen a wraith since

the missing bit

of course i couldn't understand
    what i'd known from the beginning
to comprehend the land i come from
    would have been to embellish
a head on collision
    between methuselah and malthus
would have been to meander
    with marx thru the marks
    and scratches and furrows
of the stolen if almost comprehended
    countryside

"give me your poor and huddled masses"
    that i may give them
    what was never mine to give
    or theirs to take

there was that conversation
    with raff at the ad agency
    circa january 1970
he went to the be-ins
    like the rest of us
nice young man   he was in love
with an airline stewardess - - - flying high

he confided in me that he thought
that his national guard unit
would be called up

"don't go" i said

"but that would ruin my career"

"look, raff' i said "if you get killed in a war that would ruin your
career too. and your being coerced into coercion - some fool
would have called that courage."

actually i knew better than to argue.
i had for the time left my occasional stutter behind -
the exploding dum-dums
of what i had chosen not to see
of what i had needed not to hear
which i tell not here

in december i had been told
that if i wanted to keep my job
i'd have to finish a ph d
in <u>business</u> stat of all things

that would have killed my poetry
so i gave notice - was set to sail in march
- - - in the event sailed in april - - -
lost some pension rights thru a secret glitch
was out of touch in may when kent state happened

it couldn't have happened anyhow -
    could it?
it's the missing link in the chain that mocks
    me and locks me
into american diaspora

it's the missing bit that bites into my mouth
the tale beyond telling beyond yelling the song beyond singing
the searching with neither end nor beginning
the traveller having left
the home he never had

<u>too many wizards spoil the sooth</u>

in a century
patched together with the flimsiest
 of dreams
another of those ordinary visionaries and i
raged against each other
without raising a word

the thing is it is necessary to recognise
that if you only have
 a half a dozen or so
 conflicting truths
 you're doing good

anyhow my parallel friend
despite having died some years ago
hovers in the worldwind
outside my door

<u>because i could not stop
for emily dickinson</u>

they used to have a saying
in post offices in new york -
"throw it on the fragile pile"

the fragile pile actually
is all the way over here
in the future of then
in the future

in the broom closet of xanadu
where we ponder dots over i's
the implications of crossing t's z's 7's ...
breaking words with dawn
hyphen seven   hyphen eight

maybe it's art
in any case it's less harmful
than a necklace of satellites
scouring the gobi desert
for suitable materials
to manufacture plastics
to realize the market
in vegetarian quills

<u>these are the times</u>

these are the times
of noah and gilgamesh
this is our electro-
hydraulic world

these are the times
when dante and beatrice
go see horror movies
for light relief

these are the times
when everything is
quoted out of context

when candelabra are inverted
and pressed into service
as flow charts

these are the times
of all times

nothing is new
but the most
vibrant nothing
imaginable

these are the times

note on pattern, understanding
and that sort of thing

i did not understand
the surreal evenings
at columbia university
department of statistics

i was an outsider
an observer of a forbidden world
thought myself clever
with a smattering of analysis
of variance and covariance

but this was another
universe of discourse – ORSTAT
acronym for order statistics
like a lit teacher
beating out time
or an r'n'b musician
on a pilgrimage to limerick

"how do you <u>use</u> this?"
   i asked the teacher
   at the end of a session
"oh you want to <u>use</u> it"
   he said in his
   upper class manner
that's all he said

the strange thing is that things stand still
quicker than we can move

<u>old woman in synagogue</u>

"the horizon lies open,
   messenger of no message" - - osip mandelstam

she was incredibly old, that woman
indeliberately old she seemed
she seemed as old as the earth itself, older
furrowed by centuries
of rainfall and tears

but then what did i know –
i would have preferred to have had
my bar mitzvah and its antecedent lessons
at the pentecostalike storefront shul
nearer home with its hand-clapping
klezmaniacal renditions of the old hymns
whose meanings resided in the music

i was the kid who walked all the way
to the library just off kings highway
   to read pamphlets like
frederich engels' "origin of the family,
   private property and the state"
ruth benedict's "races of mankind"
or that magical little manifesto
by marx and engels
but did not want to go that far
for my bar mitzvah
distances having to do anyhow
with the mind

so we compromised on one of the shuls in between
and on the other side of the aisle
from scrubbed and shaven males
with yarmulkas and talliseem
were the women
was that woman who i really hadn't noticed before
owing to her being so incredibly old

you have to know something about the torah
about the prohibitions against idolatry
about the sanctity of words
comprehended or not
felt
inherent in all journeys
beyond moontouch
uncreatable
being

you have to know
that the torah in a synagogue
is parchment on a scroll
on two dark wooden handles
and clothed in rich blue
decorated velvet
and each of the handles
may wear a crown
of silver filigree
you have to have walked as far
as that old woman
who was incredibly old
and it being shabbos
she couldn't ride

it could have been koran
or the tibetan chronicle
or cree or swahili ...
as it happened it was torah
and that incredibly old woman
could have been the mother
of the entire universe
could have been great-great-grandmother
to lilith adam eve
could have left the stedtl
or escaped from a nazi death-camp

the torah was carried down the aisle –
men and boys touched the fringes
of their talliseem to the torah
and then demurely touched
the fringes of the talliseem to their lips

but the incredibly old woman
ran into the aisle
and threw her arms around the torah
on that unforgettable saturday i'm recalling now
threw her arms around the torah
like it was her long-lost lover and it was
threw her arms around the torah sobbing
kissing its blue velvet cloak without restraint

can you imagine it ?
all that fuss about a book.

<u>driftwood</u>

it was my lucky day
the party was over
the party had splintered
all those break-ups
        in the space of a few months
i was 28
        was it <u>always</u> gonna be like that
obviously it wasn't
        cuz i got this job
                as a result of oversleeping
that job came in
        to the state employment
        minutes before i arrived
and as was hardly ever the case
        i was suitable
the pay was low but it was a job

you got paid every two weeks
        to make it seem like more
and then i saw it
in a store window
just about the most elegant
        shape i'd ever seen
rich brown color – polished
lacquered maybe

imagine falling in love
with a piece of wood
shaped by the sea –
i reserved it
came in once every two weeks
and made a little payment on it

i haven't got a clue
      where it is now
washed by oceans
      cast about by storms
i hadn't even <u>heard</u>
      of driftwood back then

i knew i had to have it
i knew it would console me
i knew it would shine
      like a light in my tiny room

maybe i knew
      i'd be cast about myself
imperfect   gnarled

then coming to rest
with this three dimensional
      image in my mind
and every detail of it
      that i couldn't possibly convey

i could do worse
      than to be like that piece of driftwood

i could do worse
than to bring some comfort
in a storm tossed world

that reminds me

she sez i leave the story hanging
i don't ... usually ... want to
i do my best
but sometimes, most of the time i guess
there's some detail i
have to fill in
or the narrative
would not have the coherence
that reality, whatever that is,
itself lacks

i want to tell the story
straightforwardly   as a simple act of love
like in the old days
when we were under fire
just for being ourselves
whoever we were

how d'y'tell some one
y' love her
without getting all gushy

without getting that space ship
y'call yer mind
encrusted with barnacles
parentheses, cliff-hangers reminiscent
of movie serials

with a world so full of words
so silent of echoes
how do you say it

another one of those flying lessons

i saw birds again
thru the back window
thru the unseasonal cold
thru the ironic cold
that doesn't appear to shiver
that shrugs its wings
at global warming
at power hungry
washington politicians
that fluffs its feathers
that pecks at infinitesimal bugs
on the barren branches
that enigmatically ignores
some cat stalking something in the hedge below

the ones i saw earlier today were bright
had managed to get up before i did
well i don't know where they sleep
ask an ornithologist, not some ignorant poet
but the ones i saw earlier on
were brightly colored
blue tits maybe, thrushes maybe
i couldn't tell at this distance
with my fading vision
anyhow birds unlike people
don't really seem to need to know their names
- the ones i saw later in the still brightness
were darker, more authoritative in a way
not worried about bird flu or cuckoos' nests
or you name it

must be nice to be a bird ...
and take the short view

24th Hour

i spend 23 hours a day
trying to understand why
things are the way they are

given the zillions of nows
that are possible
here-now is all there is now-here
y'know i reckon leibnitz said something like that
which made him very much
persona non grata at newton's court

but then perhaps newton was jealous of leibnitz's notation
all of which does not appear to have anything to do
with today the way i find it

the only country

the only country i can call my own
exists only in my soul nestled among
sacred memories of universe-producing
first approximations.

whenever a time or a place seems ideal
or almost ideal, for some reason or
other, it is immediately changed.

whatever nectar draws the bees
to the quangle wangle's hat has got
to be bad for business. you can
make book on that.

don't forget. the board of directors
or the soviet of angels or some-
thing or other has met.

that bird there, disappearing over
the flameless blameless horizon ... you know the bird
that doesn't exist ... i even hear
that towns are named after it –
you know, the phoenix ...

see how elegantly the invisible bird flies
and with what inspiration ...

<u>inexactly concentric circles</u>

they had a word with her
words
a phrase of praise
the poetic inscription at her feet

i don't know whether y'still can
but you used to be able to see her
from the platform of the smith-ninth street station
    upstairs from the gowanus canal
large lady in her fashionable
spiky hat

i don't know whether y'still can
but you used to be able
to look out thru her eyes
or even her crown

i hear they gave her a doctorate of letters –
y'would have thought they could have
stretched the syllabus to include syllables at least
or whole phrases, stanzas, volumes
sounds
doctor of sounds
sounding the depths
of long island sound

<u>page</u>

i sold grandma the winning raffle ticket –
she won a table top black and white
television set purely by chance

well not purely cuz y'had to have
a ticket to win
and twenty-five cents to buy a ticket

it helped to have a grandchild
from whom you bought a ticket
to humor the kid y'know - - -

after grandma died
i saw that television in the kitchen
in my parents house

i hardly ever watch television myself
- maybe once every two or three years
it requires too little attention

<u>before dawn</u>

there's this septuagenarian
     dude i never really
         expected to call myself
hobbles downstairs to brew coffee
      turn on heaters   look outside
      to see what the weather is doing
in case the wind and rain
      are not just the rustle of me
      wrestling with shadows of
      shadows of shadows of shadows
but perhaps some beleaguered intrusive cat
      seeking access, i open the door
      for just a moment, walking stick
      in hand
the cat ... seems to decide that caution
      is the better part of wisdom
      retreats until the door is closed
      again before resuming its
      other-worldly song
john sez dog-ears are a compliment
      evidence that those often turned
      corners of the spirit are not
      as lonely as they sometimes seem
he's right of course
nevertheless   meanwhile
my compliments to the cat
with its vanishing imploding disappearing song
its blakian shivers in the pregnant night

slow boil

oh, yeah, justice
wasn't she from ithica
a student at cornell perhaps

you could imagine
she had a hard time
finding her way to classes
what with the blindfold
and all that didgeridoo

a scale is meant
to tip suddenly –
not just plop
to the floor

you wonder why no one helped her
use the double edged sword
to remove the möbius blindfold

all sorts of things
that have been working their way
towards consciousness for 36 years
leapt into the light
in the night especially during the power failure

thereby no longer requiring expression
or even permitting of it

imagine waiting in a queue for 36 years
with enlightenment palpable
and all you do is make a cup of coffee

swirl

it wasn't all that often
that you got to see a squirrel anymore
even back there
where i came from
where my parents went to
for the time being the center
of the chaotic empire
where you'd expect to see anything
as all rodents lead there

oh yeah, i remember squirrels
from when i was a kid –
they hung out in parks ...
eventually frightened away i guess
by be-ins love-ins
peace demonstrators
hari-krishna chanters
much too crowded for any
self-respecting squirrel –
and i didn't even notice at the time

squirrels were part
of the landscape of my dreams –
i met with them when grandma
took me to the park
back before parks were so crowded
when people went into the planetarium
near the park
for vague hints of other worlds

squirrels were grey
that's the color squirrels were
you didn't even think about it
it was a given
they lived in memory
they lived in dream
they were grandma's entourage

and then one year i crossed the ocean
and that was close to four decades ago now
and
well about three quarters of that time ago
i saw a squirrel
near a defunct tin mine near penzance
the only squirrel i've seen
for an age and a day
and it was red
and i hadn't even known
that kind existed

now they want to have a cull
of immigrant grey squirrels ...
i was wakened by a howling wind
by turbulent dreams of recycled news reports
by recollections of a north of england
lady in vienna who
in i don't recall what context
referred to squirrels as swirls

they are debating in parliament
as to whether squirrels should be armed
and enlisted
in the malthus brigade

absence makes the heart

> "some misunderstanding is also part
> of understanding" — toru takemitsu

these deadlines throw me lifelines
self-contradiction being
in the essence of their butness
spiders facing vacuums
thoughtlessly heralding impending spring
daffodils bursting out of mist-touched
moon caressed ground
more to do than can be done
sunshine holding discourse
with blake and copernicus
some misunderstanding inevitable
as we blindly claw our many paths
toward countless stars
in uncountable skies

absense makes the heart

> "some misunderstanding is also part
> of understanding" – toru takemitsu

these deadlines throw me lifelines

self-contradiction being

in the essence of their butness

spiders facing vacuums

thoughtlessly heralding impending spring

daffodils bursting out of mist-touched

moon caressed ground

more to do than can be done

sunshine holding discourse

with blake and copernicus

some misunderstanding inevitable

as we blindly claw our many paths

toward countless stars

in uncountable skies

hokusai pie

actually the sky
is an allegorical construct
having no objective
existence at all

take this morning's sky for example
you say it's blue –
OK, grab a fistful of it . . .
now open your hand
and show it to me

see – it's no longer blue –
it was blue . . . it's blown - - -
this analysis of the sky thing
has blown it

it'll blow over tho –
elijah will blow into town
things will settle
or rise
into the skies
that comprise
the allegorical actuality
of the sky

<u>on the sexuality of god</u>

the walls of herself protected me
she read the books and
     oh they were various
the letters broke off words
     and fell pell mell
this was a new country
had i perhaps been begotten
     for company
her partner in all of this
     was undiscernable in his raging
they the others
     modeled whomsoever sat in the
        sky on him – impossible ...
anyone with any sense
     knows a god has to be female

<u>the evolution of poetry</u>

the first poem
   our leader

the second poem
   our leader is the best
   our leader is one of the gods
   and makes us free

the third poem
   we carve likenesses
   of our leader
   who delegates the best among us
   to imprison those of us who assert
   that come to think of it
   we are not free

the fourth poem
   we uncover that our leader
   is the only god and
   therefore invisible so
   we smash his icons
   which we when in chains
   fashioned and wander
   in deserts following the
   tails of comets

the fifth poem
   we are incarcerated
   as icon smashers
   we learn crafts of recording
   fashion factions
   splinter fractions
   express disatisfaction

with our universe which
    being perfect
    has a complaint department
    which never shuts

the sixth poem
    the prisons having burst
    at the seams
    the very old and the very young
    under house arrest
    the fittest among us
    although not necessarily
    the most wise or the best
    will in the name of our leader
    our god our conception
    our way of life
    carry freedom on the end
    of a sword
    to the infinite numbered
    corners of the cornerless
    universe

the seventh poem
    consists in
    debates about suitable meters
    and scripts and languages
    and musics and meanderings
    and manynesses and nuances
    of

the first poem
    our leader

loaf

i am not that kid
i don't recall his name
    if i ever knew it
for one thing i'm much too old
    to have been that kid
maybe twice his age at the time
– for another – as far as i can
    discern – i'm not nearly as
    clever as that kid was

i seem to remember – now remembering
    that time or what happens over
    time or thru the agency of time
    or whatever metamorphoses mental
    oils into watercolors –
    in some sense blurs
but let's look thru the astigmatic
    lens of a few decades nevertheless

he had attended or was attending
the same high school i had gone to
a science high school in downtown manhattan
took an hour to get there from
    remote parts of brooklyn

the paper that he was reading
    or that someone was reading
    on his behalf
was about a number system
of his own invention
or discovery
based on an irrational base

i am not that boy
nor rachmaninoff
nor toscanini

i am part of the same species
being a person   i'm an object
being a foreign person
    i'm a foreign object
i thrive on alienation

just when i think
    i'm finding out who i am
    it changes

funny thing about life
it hurts but it's
goddamn interesting

<u>tentative conclusion in six quatrains</u>

something awoke
maybe tomorrow
maybe yesterday
i'm not sure

it awoke as from a dream
it rubbed its eyes
it looked at skies
thru skipping rope rainbows

it said so many of us
have wrestled with this
it's bigger than all of us
this nothingness they sing of

yes as you approach
the reciprocal of zero
from above or below
it becomes plus or minus infinity

this divergence could shatter
as you approach it
from a continuous infinitude
of other directions

see that elegant pawprint in the sky
i did that
digging digging digging
trying to understand

RIDING THE CAROUSEL HORSE

"... if i can ride my horse,
and get there, then I'm
absolutely sure.........."
- D. H. Lawrence

"Heaven that never was
Nor will be ever is always true,"
- Dylan Thomas

The carousel horse had run away. Oh the times he had dreamed of the carousel horse running away, of it taking to the sky like the red flying horse on Mobiloil was it and of the commercials on Saturday afternoon's Metropolitan Opera radio broadcasts. Uncle Stephen had muttered something about (what was it now) Penitence or Peneus - something about some Greek horse that sounded something like penis. Anyhow, here in his technicolor reverie, the carousel horse had run away and Coney Island opened into the sky and God sat in a clown suit with red and green paint on His jolly face. All he had done was to grab the brass ring as the horse whirled past it and actually caught it and pulled and instead of the ring just coming into his hand it stayed there and pulled back a galaxy as he tugged at it. So this was freedom. The carousel horse had run away.

He loved his visits with his mother to Mrs. Maxwell's house and strangely associated them with the mysteries of Beethoven and Shostakovich who came wafting over radio station WQXR on the Maxwell House Coffee Hour ... those visits ... they were ... like in the commercial ... "good to the last drop." He wasn't quite sure what a widow was ... knew a black widow was a dangerous spider who ate her husband but Mrs. Maxwell didn't have a husband - just Arthur and herself and an old old old father - well, he thought he must be her father because his name was Mr. Maxwell and he lived there and Arthur called him "grandpa" and Mrs. Maxwell took care of him. Arthur was seven and they usually played together but Arthur wasn't home today and he liked that better because he could explore alone while his mother and Mrs. Maxwell talked out on the porch. He could envelop himself in the magic room. It was difficult being away from Mr. Maxwell whom he admired and thoroughly intended to be when he himself was old. As his mother and Mrs. Maxwell talked, the old man just rocked faster and faster in his wicker rocking chair out there on the porch, unrepentantly passing wind with a loud explosion each time the wicker arc rocked through a particular invisible point in its curvilinear trajectory. These explosions were declarations of independence, of not giving a damn for social convention, of being as free and defiant as nature itself. They were, to the boy, more musical than Elgar's Land of Hope and Glory. But today, with Arthur away - where (?) at some never-mentioned relative - today, with Arthur away, the boy could hear a different music at the periphery of the magic room.

What made the room magic was the window. Windows were for looking out into the street or the garden - down at the men with pneumatic drills or the robins herding worms near the honeysuckle bush ... other windows, that is, but this window was different. It looked in. It faced the <u>other</u> room, the room with the strange odor of powdered lilacs ... the room that was the echo of Mrs. Maxwell. And looking out of a window into a room was a strange sensation. Half a lifetime later, constructing some poetic memoir, he was to write, "Uncle Truth was eight years old and his name was me. He looked in out of windows and that was a metaphysical statement." He was to write that on a note pad in a rocking chair while rocking violently and passing explosions of wind into a honeysuckled breeze. Actually, he had been six. His mother had met Mrs. Maxwell at the kindergarten PTA when he was five. He had cried so bitterly at being left at kindergarten but now his family had moved and he went to a different school and, since it was worse, he didn't cry any more.

He tiptoed into the room beyond the window as he had done before and went unerringly to the ornate little box that was the source of the lilac-like smell and opened it as he had done before and listened as he had done before to the tinkling music of the Merry Widow Waltz and closed his eyes and was on a carousel where a somewhat brassier version of the same melody had been played or cranked out by mechanical means last summer. His horse was black with red ornamentation. The bridle was red. The saddle was red and gold. He daydreamed of the horse and of his mental communication with a cosmic gang of other boys exactly like himself scattered through the galaxy, thinking exactly his thoughts, riding carved wooden horses exactly like his carved wooden horse ... black and red and red and gold - through fields of powdered lilac or was it lavender or was it just the magic aroma of the romantic secrets of Mrs. Maxwell. He felt a strange sensual tingle, not yet defined or localized - perhaps a little wicked, perhaps very holy.

And then he went to Arthur's room and it was there. It hadn't been there before. A rocking horse. Chestnut colored with brown and lavender ornamentation although the boy was to remember a black rocking horse with red and gold ornamentation. He got on the horse and rocked and rocked and rocked and closed his eyes and rocked faster and faster and faster and became old Mr. Maxwell and became the ghost that caressed Mrs. Maxwell's mysterious merry widow lilac lavender death life love scent in that mystical room beyond the window that looked inward into his soul and outwards into the entire universe and he rocked and rocked and dreamed that he flew and flew in his mind and climbed out of himself and lay on the royal blue rug with its border of tiny rosebuds and looked up at the horse still rocking and saw the carousel horse, the horse of every ecstatic explosion that was to sustain him in worlds of grimness and despair and bombs and pneumatic drills so that when he went home with his mother later that afternoon after milk and cookies, he was a different person and contained more treasure than the Hope Diamond - namely hope itself. The carousel horse had run away.

THE SOLOMON OF THE GUTTER

After peace, came war. In retrospect, the peace could not be remembered; only inferred... the many naps in the years that followed, head buried under quilt and between pillows suggestive of that dark, warm, quiet time that ironically had begun with an explosion of what an Austrian psychoanalyst who was to die in an American prison was to liken to atomic energy. Considering the words that were to fall like hailstones on his naked heart, it would be inconceivable if he were conceived in love. Yet peace ensued. Or in any case, a nine month truce.

Then came a second explosion... the beginning of the war. Like the peace that preceded it, the opening battle could only be inferred. It was deducible from one of the recurrent nightmares that marred his childhood. It was the spider who told him of his terrible birth - not in words, for a new born baby does not know words, but in the nature of its being. He was enveloped in a glass bubble which in turn was enveloped in the visceral legs of the spider. He was trapped, broke the glass and it bled, tore through the enclosing viscera only to find himself in another, larger bubble, enveloped by a larger spider, breaking out again and then again and then again, his iterated escape frustrated and frustrated and frustrated until at last he screamed himself awake, crying again like a new born baby who had torn his way into the world. A well known poet has written that you cannot be born too often. The spider's child was to be born again and again and again yet always feeling not yet born.

It was not until he was an adult and the spider nightmares had ceased that his mother told her side of the story. She put it this way. It was the hottest day of the year. She too was a prisoner. (How often after that had he been a willing prisoner, turning to a tyranny of love or work or whatever, wanting it to be the warm dark dungeon he had lived in before this cruel and tendentious expulsion into the light - almost unable to go forward, entirely unable to go back?) She was incarcerated in a maternity ward where, as fashion had it, deliverance was to take place.

Air conditioning did not yet exist and it was the hottest day of the year. She was deeply drugged and, through her, he was, which accounted for the need to struggle to accomplish what unfettered nature usually accomplishes with ease. Because of the whim of an artistic king in another country in another time, she was flat on her back. She lay on a rubber sheet and the amniotic fluid mingled as freely with perspiration as with blood. She screamed. He screamed. The entire universe screamed. The July sun burned the urban sky. From the warm sweet dungeon in which he had been serenaded by her heartbeat, he was born into a world of screams.

In a very real sense, he was the child of an abstract principle. Behaviourism. It decreed that he was a man before he was a child. And although, for a limited time - until its presumed sudden termination - she gave him the milk and warmth of her breasts, it was strictly a matter of schedule, a rigidity which was to doom him to decades and decades of obsession with schedules and calendars, work plans and clocks. Whenever he cried for milk and love before the allotted time, his father forcibly restrained his mother... made her wait until the time when the sacred theory said that he could cuddle and feed. His upbringing was as far from natural tribal intuition as the city he lived in was from any natural landscape. He was the son of theory.

I have said he could not have been conceived in love. His mother, in her groping, blinded, heartbreaking way, loved him. His father hated him even before he was born. I have proof of this not only in his father's behaviour towards him from the very start but in the very language that his father used. "You smell like the pestilence," his father would say, although he smelled no different than anyone else. "You are the dirtiest boy on the block," and innocently, the boy would believe that an actual survey had been taken. "You are so lazy, you stink." The boy was hardworking and inquisitive. "Vomit yourself out," when inconveniently and to his father's great annoyance, the boy, not surprisingly, stuttered. These were just a few of the milder insults.

There are no records of when he was weaned, but considering the spiritual climate of the time, the incipient fascism, the dominance of behaviourism in its first flush, his father's cold, autocratic fire, his mother's typically petit bourgeois slavishness in following the cook books of the soul, we can infer that he was weaned early, suddenly and well before the initial fracture from which all the tributary cracks were to follow - like chasms in a desert of rock - like waterless rivers. If like Moses he was to see a land of milk and honey from a distance, it was to be like Moses from a parched and arid Sinai stuffed with dead commandments. That fracture had a pre-history as I have suggested, short in arithmetical terms but logarithmic in intensity and the turning point of those earliest days was the bursting of the dam of language... the emergence of the feared and adored Unreal Tongue. For his parents, although already petit bourgeois in aspiration, were as yet proletarian immigrants in a strange land and spoke their own language to him until suddenly as he began to master it another language was substituted and he was never to feel real again. The change was abrupt and when, defensively, he fell in love with the new language and embraced it, it was withdrawn and inducements such as chocolates were offered to woo him back to the old language, the language which had driven his parents into exile. Years later, himself an immigrant in the world his parents had abandoned, but not yet returned to the countryside of their peasant roots, he lived for a while enveloped in the long-forgotten first language. There in the heart of what had once been the Austro-Hungarian Empire, amid the revving of the motorcycles, a giant sign above a Gothic landscape bore the word KLAVIER which chilled him and resonated among the chords of the secret piano of his heart. He had nightmared this very same Gothic landscape months before actually seeing it - had dreamed that he ran mad through the streets of Vienna. But the fracture, the initial fracture I speak of, occurred long before that, perhaps a year and a half after this presumably sudden weaning when, with equal suddenness and no warning, a mask was pushed onto his face and a group of towering adults pushed him into the ethereal world of ether, in his unconsciousness to assault him and extract an organ from his throat. In keeping with the behaviourofascism of the time, his parents had been despatched to a movie and he had been given no warning of the terror that was to befall him, a terror he was to seek out in later years to attempt to resolve and defang under the influence of chosen drugs and hypnosis and nostalgic nausea on the banks of the lysergic river. Through all those earlier terrors, his grandmother was to sustain him, his gateway to the past. Later, stories of gas chambers were to strike chords beyond the realms of conscious apprehension.

In school, they taught him how to read time. After hours he fled from it. There were cats underneath the cars and he wished to converse with them. He crawled under the cars, imitating the auto mechanics he had admired and envied... again the exhaust pipes suggestive of some fumes holding secrets of life and death... he did get dirty, perhaps not quite verbalising the idea that it was as well to be hung for a sheep as for a lamb. He had little to say to most boys - their violence offended him - sought the company of girls... willingly played house, played gynecologist, used his grandfather's discarded cigar bands to marry every girl he met. He was the sultan of the alley, the Solomon of the gutter.

THE FEAR OF RAPE

The year is 1933, the year of Hitler, the year of the National Recovery Administration, the year Japan withdraws from the League of Nations. The young boy, like all children, like all of us, the child of a history he cannot choose, is firmly clamped over the rim of the bathtub, the rim grinding into his gut, clamped into place by his father's muscular arms while his mother thrusts the long object with its vaseline-clogged perforations into his anus, the involuntarily tightening sphincter muscles creating a paroxysm of pain. The clamp on the tube is released and the warm water from the uplifted rubber bag gushes into his innards creating pressure and pain. The pressure must be maintained as long as possible. The pain must be endured. The water must be retained despite its blinding jabs until the precise moment when he is permitted to dash to the toilet and release it along with the undigested white bread and other matter imprisoned in his gut. Regularity is essential. The assembly line must be maintained. There is duty to perform. The trains must run on time. The water clock is ticking ... it is the body and soul of a little boy.

A box of soap suppositories lies on the shelf next to a box of luxury condoms. The enema is not a nightly resort but used only when the suppositories fail to produce the desired result, They are painful enough but the boy lies across the rim of the bathtub voluntarily in hopes of avoiding the greater evil of the internal whirlpool. This is free will. It is similar to the electoral process. It is 1933. Japanese troops are committing atrocities in Manchuria. It is possible that some of these may entail an enema.

A car is waiting in front of the apartment building. It is Sunday, a time for visiting relatives. It is summer and a small boy is wearing a white short-sleeved shirt and short white trousers, a brown belt and white and brown shoes. Also a brown Eton hat. The boy is waiting downstairs, in front of the apartment building, under the marquee.

The car ride is to be well over an hour and he is not to disrupt it with requests to go to the toilet, which would necessitate his father leaving the highway and driving hither and thither in search of a parking place with a suitable amenity, cursing Sunday drivers, crowded road conditions, delay in general, the car in particular, his son for being so bothersome, his wife for "interfering" when he subjects the boy to a tongue-lashing for being so awkward and difficult. Before he was permitted to go downstairs, his mother had asked him had he gone to the toilet. "Yes," he said, but admitted shamefacedly that he had not moved his bowels. "But did you strain?" his mother asked. "Yes," he had dutifully replied. Now he was in front of the house and had been ordered under no circumstances to come back up while his parents are trying to get ready to go; it was late enough already. He is in front of the house and a cramp is occurring. He represses it. He dare not go upstairs. He might even take one elevator while his parents take the other and miss them, coming to an empty apartment, continuing up and down all day, missing them each time, disrupting their social calendar, and their precious Sunday, now his father is working six days a week, seven sometimes, setting up his own business to provide the better things of life, to provide a life worth living with all the material comforts and all the suppositories and condoms and loaves of white bread and a shiny new toaster in the kitchen and a refrigerator instead of an ice box despite the depression. The boy struggles and then can struggle no more as one squishy lump and then another forms in his short trousers, one lump falling to the pavement, another discoloring the trousers, forming a white and brown pattern similar to that on the shoes. The boy waits, still terrified of taking the wrong elevator. People pass him in their Sunday finery. His gaze rooted to the ground, he kicks his turd to a tree, next to one left there by a dog. Then his parents come. There are shouts, screams, accusations, slaps. He is pulled by the ear and by the arm, thrown into the shower upstairs with his clothing still on, the shower turned on high like some vengeful enema raining down celestial fury from above, the needle-like streams of water stinging the exposed portions of his skin, hammering his clothing against him. He gasps, fearful that he cannot breathe, that he will drown in the shower and die disgraced, covered with water and excrement. It is 1933. Germany withdraws from the League of Nations. The United States recognises the Soviet Union and diplomatic relations between Washington and Moscow resume.

It is 1945. Roosevelt dies. American troops and Russian troops meet at the River Elbe. A teenager with diarrhea darts into a cafeteria, runs to an unoccupied booth, closes the door, tears open his trousers, flings himself onto the seat and explodes, sits awhile resting, touching himself, dazed, glances up and there is a hole about an inch wide in the cubicle wall just near the toilet roll holder and an eye is in it ... watching him. The boy gasps, hastily wipes himself, pulls up his trousers, darts out of the toilet without washing his hands, terrified of being accosted by the watcher. It is 1945. American airplanes dump death on the cities of Hiroshima and Nagasaki.

It is 1946. Korea is partitioned between the US and the USSR. Juan Perón becomes president of Argentina. American atom bombs are dropped on Bikini Atoll. A young man is being examined by his draft board in the gymnasium of a high school named for a medieval academic. The doctor has already listened to his heart, taken his blood pressure, tested his vision, looked into his eyes, ears, nose, throat, caused him to gag on a tongue depressor, placed two fingers under his testicles and told him to cough. And now is the real assertion of authority. The doctor, a thick condom-like sheath on his finger, plunges it roughly into the anus of the young man, like a thick suppository or a dry enema. "Ow," the young man mutters, biting his lower lip. "You'll do," the doctor says, "1A." It is 1946. Peace has begun. The United Nations has been formed. There are civil wars in China, Indo-China and Greece.

It is 1949. NATO is established. The Russians explode their own atom bombs. The two Germanies are set up. A young university student is worried about the draft .... I'll do anything to stay out. Guy like me, no good at baseball or anything, bound to be raped, bound to be invaded (nightmares of steamtrains hurtling up his anus) guy like me ... keep a switchblade under my pillow, know what the army is, what it's like, guy tries to rape me, I'll cut his throat, self-defence ... be locked up for it, maybe shot. Just won't go in the army, no matter what .... It is 1949. The Nationalist Chinese government escapes to Taiwan. India prepares to declare its independence.

It is 1950. The Korean War has begun. A telegram is on the table, saying "Greetings." A young man has been drafted. An empty bottle of pills is on the table. A young man is dead. It is 1950. Pope Pius XII proclaims the dogma of the Assumption of the Virgin.

AN ASSIGNATION WITH LADY TRUTH

Vera, I cannot come to the mountain. They arrested me at the development, for an obscene passage in my sacred symphony and interred me in a soulless condominium studded with proletarian emeralds in a market research gulag of spiritual decay. Vera, they caught me in possession of my faculties. Vera, I cannot come to the mountain.

Vera, I cannot come to the mountain. Business affairs detain me. I stood next to Ginsberg at the swami's birthday party and did not speak, refused an introduction to Auden, then read his Herod on a stormy sea, watching dolphins in the sunshine when the turbulence subsided, was nearly placed in the nest of the lyrebird by a wealthy lady but then she committed suicide, muffed contracts, deals, which in any case I was not ready for. The gem was not yet polished. I have painted the sunshine and now I am blind.

Vera, I cannot come to the mountain. I have filed briefs and papers, recorded every irrelevant detail demanded by the high court of finance, discovered the liberation of poverty, sat in the auroral glow of atomic disintegration counting stamps, watching the postbox. listening to the silence of the telephone, fitting with five-penny pieces the four corners of my chariot, wailing to Apollo to take me riding with the sun. I freed myself from the bondage of dollars and chained myself with pennies.

Vera, I cannot come to the mountain. I never have calendar and engagements at the same time. My fingers are packed with typographical errors and transpositions. The binding of my dictionary is broken and the words come flooding out. I must plug the dike with my own body. Children are screaming in the street and they hate each other. The baby next door cries in the bath and does not want to be cleansed and cleansed of the sacred perspiration of enlightenment. Vera, I am angry. Vera, I am mad. Vera, I cannot come to the mountain.

Vera, I cannot come to the mountain because of the hailstorm, because of my inefficiency, because the world has cracked, because my ears are bleeding, because you and the mountain know too much, because I am guilty, because I am innocent, because in Nevada the desert is rising, because the oppressed are oppressed, because the oppressed rise up and become the oppressor. Vera, understand me, I cannot come to the mountain.

Vera, I cannot come to the mountain. There is nowhere I can go without my medals. There is too much cruelty on the road to Damascus and I cannot be a life scout in an eagle's nest. Vera, we threw him into the shower like so many nazis, we cheered for our team and were ready to die for our music. I waved the flag of my country, Vera, and I cannot remember its colors! Conscripts of lottery and deception lay dead in the meadow; what self-determination theirs? Vera, I have no shoes; I cannot come to the mountain.

Vera, I cannot come to the mountain. I await the invoice, the muse, the typewriter repairman, the computer analyst in the pagan glen, the martyr with clothes of fire, the scream of Joan, the whisper of the tree, the intimate song of the brook. There was a jailbreak today, Vera, but I cannot come to the mountain.

Vera, I cannot come to the mountain. I am tired of talking, insomniac, satiated with sleep, fearful of food and all the poisons of my century, ashamed of the sins of the ancestors. The Bible and the Koran stand on my shelf and my entrails are full of blood.

Vera, I cannot come to the mountain. They seized me on Bedford Avenue and tore off my trousers for the crime of being new in the neighbourhood and I retaliated by seeing crystallized socially necessary surplus value like some multidimensional rock candy bursting out of the sides of consumer products. Earlier, I had been crucified on Ocean Avenue, to hang with two others, offered by hyenas as a sacrifice for the lamb and saw angels in space suits. I superimposed realities on Madison Avenue in a covariance of my soul, led wildcat job actions in Newark, New Jersey, in defense of beauty and integrity, was brought to dock by kangaroos in wigs and counterrevolutionary communists. I tried to stop a bullet in Herald Square ... the love affair ended but I still have that. The knife never connected. I was meant to be murdered by the mob in Red Hook but I think it rained that night.

I knew a millionairess copywriter who was beaten with chains. I have seen seals robbed of their fur in the name of ethnic integrity.

Vera, I cannot come to the mountain. I have seen women cry over the memories of shadows of the torments of those they did not know, have seen iron-faced politicians promise resolve, have met evasive priests and poets who are not poets and a few who are. I have seen the worm crowned. I have seen the hero disintegrate under the weight of his laurels, have heard peace lovers denounced and warriors celebrated, have seen men turn their backs on women and embrace their shoes. The church is building a superhighway to Gomorrah. How can I come to the mountain? There are bigots on every side. The mountain is blocked. Vera, I know it is not. I know you are there. But, Vera, I cannot come to the mountain.

Vera, I cannot come to the mountain. I paint pictures of the mountain. I am the mountain but cannot come to it. My book is the mountain. My body is the mountain. Vera, I am equally seduced by recognition and neglect. Singing the ultimate psalm, I embrace the irrelevant. Washing the cowshit off my hands, I knock the chalice to the floor. Vera, you know I am the humpback whale singing of rainbows in the sewer. I am a star, Vera, like all stars born of darkness.

Vera, I have nothing to tell you. Vera, why don't you answer my questions? Vera, God himself doesn't know why there is evil! Vera, why do I love you? Why do I wear the clothing of honesty when the shoes of deception are comfortable? Vera, why do you not respond to the remarks I have not made? Lies refute themselves but do so wrongly and dragons slither not from the light but from the popular phrase that is beside the point. Vera, I cannot come to the mountain because children memorize maxims, because imbeciles pass exams, because I have won a prize, because I am guilty, because I am innocent, because Galois flunked plane geometry and was killed in a duel, because someone murdered Martin Luther King, because Chagall painted a magical shade of blue.

Vera, I cannot come to the mountain because I am ill, because my intestines cry, because there are sermons in my broken arms.

Vera, I cannot come to the mountain because I am not dead. When I am dead, they will carry me to the mountain. And then you may question me all you like. But only the wind will answer.

A MOMENT OF GRACE

Grace had a wild tumble of dark brown waterfall hair atop her head and lived in a quiet isolated house just off Extremis Road. The name of the house was Negation. She had taken me into a spacious kitchen with a rear view of the sun. She opened a drawer and removed an egg-shaped stone, transparent as glass, clear and colorless inside but with a pale limpid orange-colored surface, and held it up to the picture window, and we looked in it or through it. And I was transported to the land in the mind of that glass.

In that world, I was walking with Grace and she was telling me about her childhood. "When I was six, they gave me silver stars. When I was seven they gave me gold. When I was eight, I discovered you could buy gold and silver stars in the store, and I lost my incentive." We were walking down a long grey brick road ... past four dead pigeons neatly lying along the verge. The sky was one of those brilliant Chagall blues you see in dreams and the edges of the scattered lavender clouds were sharp and clear.

I said to Grace, "I do not understand everything." And she replied, "How beautiful not to understand everything. What a blessing that we will never know and be trapped by our under-standing. Look around you. Look at those wild Van Goghs growing in the field. Men in their lust for knowledge have broken open the microworld, thereby threatening to destroy it.." The moon sang, its exploration and colonization a hallucination, an artifact of time. And beneath that silver dish hanging in the sky, I moved closer to Grace and kissed her.

When I kissed Grace, she disappeared. I continued alone along the grey brick road, beneath a darkening sky, picking flowers that had burst through the cracks in the road as I walked. The sky was growing black and ominous and the flowers were purple and orange and golden and brilliant red and all of them had thorns. Eventually, the road entered the city and then I came to the medical center and in front of the medical center was a yard full of broken automobiles and in front of that a dead pigeon. I continued through the grounds of the medical center, picking more flowers ... blue and silver and jade ... until I reached the mental hospital where screams were being bottled and head transplants were taking place and the receptionist asked me which patient I was visiting, who I wanted to see and I said "Grace." The receptionist took my flowers and threw them in a waste paper basket. "These are not permitted," she said, "We put them in vases and the patients break the vases and attack themselves and us and each other." I asked about cardboard vases and she said they weren't regulation but that I could buy more flowers in the gift shop. "What will you do with them if I do?" I asked. "Throw them in the waste basket," she replied.

When Grace came to me again, she had whirlpools in her eyes. She threw her arms around me and kissed me but an attendant rushed up and pulled her off me. "That is not per-mitted," he said. Surreptitiously, I took Grace's hand and we walked down the corridor together until we reached the room where they were having the writing workshop. Dozens of men and women of every age and description were sitting at type-writers that had been fitted with rolls of thin white wrapping paper for uninterrupted feed and as the keys struck the pages the words glowed and the very paper sang. And the papers fed out continuously into the center of the room, there being consumed in a gigantic fire. "There are of course writings that are not mad," Grace said. They are about heroes and warriors and death and honor and vengeance and movie stars and the petulance of an invisible Deity." "And where are these writings?" I asked. "Preserved among the bones and other fossils, down at the university."

I took my leave of Grace by the artists' exit at the back of the mental hospital and entered a courtyard, under a white sky, where there was a chalk drawing on the pavement of Salome in veils of seven colors and the chalk lines danced and the veils were removed and nothing was revealed and the pavement was grey and concrete. Eventually I came to the grey brick road again and continued my journey. As I walked, the sky again darkened and gradually turned indigo and a huge luminous golden ringtoss-like circle appeared in the sky and a man in flowing robes was berating strollers for adopting the wrong rituals and angering God who he said was very particular about such matters and would poison and starve their children and their children's children as punishment. Someone photographed him, and his followers stoned this person for making a graven image, because these followers were holy.

Eventually I came to a factory and in front of the main building was a dead pigeon and workers were picketing the factory demanding the restoration of their jobs and therefore their dignity. I enquired what was made at the factory and was told "gas chambers for concentration camps." They were no longer needed. People used to be transported in cattle cars to these places but now were dealt with in more efficient ways and this was progress. I heard the voice of Grace within me observing that if cattle had never been crowded together and transported for slaughter there would never have been cattle cars to transport people in, that inhumanity is incremental and as gradual as the darkening sky. A little girl sat on an empty oil drum near the factory, her face wet with tears. But the stars were shining and the little girl was singing.

I entered the song of the little girl and in the song her mother was falling about a room, banging her forehead on the window and cracking the glass, and banging the back of her head on the mirror. The room kept tilting and I fell out, back on the grey brick road, beneath a pale blue sky, streaked with red. There I met Grace and we talked about the philosophers' stone and about alchemy and science and the birth and death of the universe and about the non-utility of argument because if you have to defend yourself, there's no point in defending yourself, about the inevitability of death, the consequent fact that there is nothing really to fear, the certainty of oneness, the limitations of friendship, the curse of normalism, the quest for lost insanity, the uncluttered clarity of total alienation, the politics of despair, the despair of politics, about sad ecstasy and exuberant sorrow, about the cadaverous whore that sometimes passes for art, about joy and ambiguous surprise. She remarked that a person with no cosmic perspective is half dead and that the person with only cosmic perspective is also half dead. I marvelled at the wisdom of Grace and she asked me why I was making such a fuss about ordinary conversation. The crowd thickened and people were angry about my discourse with Grace. For this reason and because we were getting nearer to the university, Grace disappeared. My steps became slow and sluggish because the rucksack I was carrying was filled with other people's thoughts. I discarded it but was still beleaguered by the warring factions of my soul.

I came to the university at last and the main building was devoted to biological warfare and other practical pursuits expressly funded by private industry. At the cornerstone of the building, there was carved, "ERECTED BY A GRATEFUL PUBLIC. 'TO KNOW IS TO BE.'" At the base of the cornerstone lay a dead pigeon.

I went past the main building and into the campus. The sky turned deep red. The language riots between the Esperantists and the Interlinguists had begun. They hacked at each other with cleavers and there were many casualties. The parents of some of the participating students came to the university and they were grateful because all the dead bodies were returned. Used up bodies are of enormous value and comfort to the bereaved. If there is an improper event like an earthquake, they will dig the dead bodies out of the ground and dig another hole and put them back in ... properly, like they do with gold. A rock-and-roll requiem was played at the Student Union and the sky turned black. It had silver streaks as if the universe were wearing a pin-striped suit. Everything went quiet. Everything disappeared,

When the world re-appeared, I was in an orange-skied wilderness traversed by electric pylons that the wind was playing like a guitar. And then a dirt road appeared and a cherubic man was driving a tractor down it and our eyes met and it came to me that happiness was not to be sought after but sadness accepted and in the distance a river sang the blues. And I met a spirit who taught me how to fly and we flew together over oceans and swirling sands and rocky crags and barren trees and dog turd dried sculpturally by the sun and arctic tundra and brooks and lakes and convulsive mountains and neon lights and quiet glens. And then I was at the university again and the riots were over or had not yet occurred and I walked on a grey brick road under a grey brick sky past the stocks and the dunking stool and the museum and the cyclotron and the computer center and a young man on a bench destroying a flower to discover whether it loved him or loved him not and past the school of agriculture and the school of business administration and a college of cardinals preening their red feathers. And then I saw a plinth and on that plinth was a dead pigeon and I knew I was approaching the library. And I could smell the decaying books and the sky turned as clear as water.

Once in the library, I went to the reading room and there I found what seemed like hundreds of shelves and I picked a book at random off one of the shelves and took it over to a low table and sat down in an easy chair and opened the book to read and I leafed through it looking for the beginning but all the pages were blank. An old man came up to me and he looked like me and he had a wiry grey beard and thin frizzy hair falling down over his ears and he said to me, "You are obviously a man of perception." "Why do you say that?" I asked. "You are reading the only book of value in the entire university."

He told me he was the author and I asked if I could borrow the book and he said no, as it was the only copy, but he had something of equal value he had acquired shortly after a long and delayed train ride over a sea of broken ice. It had been given to him by God one day when She was feeling generous ... and he gave me a single speck of sand. It was the sand, he said, of the first birth, of no past, of no history.

"Is this to borrow or to keep?" I asked.

"It is to lose."

"Then of what value is it?"

"You will have had it."

"But that would be my history."

I had already lost the grain of sand as we were approaching the front of the library. The old man told me it didn't matter and started turning away saying, "There's a man waiting for you outside and he's growing impatient."

"How will I know him?"

"He has a tiny goatee and darting eyes."

"He made a beautiful painting once," I said, and imprisoned a woman in it, But eventually he set her free."

"She freed herself."

"He's me a long time ago."

"So is his son," my mentor replied. And then he added, as he hurried back down the corridor, "Live as if you had one year left to live." I think he returned to the reading room, possibly seeking another self. Or perhaps to the newspaper morgue.

The man with the goatee was nervous. He stood on the steps of the university library with his young son, nervous too, and both were shadowed by the greyness of the academy. The man asked me to fly with his son to a point just beyond the horizon. The son jumped and tried to lie on the air face down with his arms forward and I told him none of that was necessary. He asked me "How <u>do</u> you fly then?" and I told him you just have to lie on your back and relax and I lay down on the air and drifted quickly and easily forward with him huffing and puffing behind me in his Superman pose and we neared a place where we had to negotiate between some buildings and he asked me to do a foot turning and his voice was desperate. Gently I put my right foot out to the right and a little up and we drifted upward and rightward and past the city, back into the country again and over the roof of Negation House. I looked down over my left shoulder and saw Grace and myself looking out.

The sky was Chagall blue.

GETTING WISDOM

"And we - that dreamed youth's
blade would never rust,
Hoped wells from the mirage,
roses from the sand -
The riddle of the world
shall understand
And put on wisdom with
the robe of dust."

- Mu'tamid, King of Seville (lived 1040-95 A.D.)

It is not easy being a griffin. Half the eggs I have laid have not hatched at all and the other half have hatched not into griffins but into things ephemeral such as rainbows and movements of political liberation. In the land of the blind, the one-eyed man is ... killed. The two-eyed man does not exist. And the griffin, devoted as she is to maximum flower, is a figment of her own imagination. In the world of the griffin there is no greatness, because greatness depends upon suppression. If everyone were allowed to achieve his or her full potential, that contrast that we call greatness would be unsupportable. Einstein would be the checkout boy at your supermarket. Accordingly, there would be no bomb and such madnesses as prevail in your universe - star wars, monetarism, advanced food technology - would be unable to come into being, much less persist. And people would have to make do with smaller fantasies and would revert to conjuring talking griffins with their minds. I exist in a world that is not, shining a light into the world that is. I am a griffin. The crea-ture of play. The wild dolphin of the air. But unlike the dolphin, I am sad. The dolphin is happy because she is lacking in information. I, being your fantasy, know all.

I wasn't always this way. I wasn't always a griffin. I was a normal little girl but grew up into adulthood with an awareness that what you call reality is merely that mythology that maximises predictability. As such, as the Greek tragedians know, it has little actual utility. Watch the lambs grazing and you will notice that the survival value of having a broad picture is minimal. Sufficient unto the day, if you're a lamb. They don't anticipate. They are non-political. But I was too headstrong to be a lamb. Too filled with longing. Too fantastic. Too sexual. I abandoned reality and flew into the sky of my own wonderings.

I flew with Pegasus and was his wife, fed the hungry for there is more than enough food in the world, disintegrated irrelevant matter with my thoughts and purchased freedom with my cries, assumed human form to mate with Gregory Corso, went back in time and lived with Methuselah, retreated further into the mists and guarded the young of the pterodactyl, swam into the future and shuddered with the madness of realisation as I encountered the vapidity of my genetically engineered double, collapsed into a world of melted suns and dissolute chronometers. In dreams I sat on crags overlooking boiling oceans. I saw frozen mountains shatter. I learned that suicide in the realest sense is impossible since we are all all and that all is all that might be ... that the tragedy is irrepressible and that her name is music. There is no guarantee of anything except the transcendent self. When you <u>know</u> you're locked up, you're in some sense free. And then again, you never are. I heard a young man with a guitar singing once, "Sylvie brought me coffee. Sylvie brought me tea. She brought me nearly every damn thing. But she didn't bring the jailhouse key."

In the court of the medieval king of Seville, I wrote a poem and called it "My Sister's Serenade." The king, a poet himself, did not regard it as a poem but a thousand years hence he would have. But he did acknowledge that it had something. Translated from the original Arabic, it went like this:

"Hello, beautiful tree
Your numerous elegantly sculpted branches
Holographically silhouetted in indigo air
Singing silently the mathematics of love -
Tree, unaware of me
And (lacking centrality) unaware of yourself –
The being that transcends knowing

Polymorphous unperversely
Implicit in every twig and bud ...
An entire forest
An entire universe
Every conceivable eon
Present in one eyeblink apprehension
Of one beautiful tree."

After I wrote that, I wrote a novel riding on a roller coaster. I spent five minutes translating the Koran into Swedish but took ten years with a single painting. I was not afraid to undertake projects but lived one day at a time. I rocked skyscrapers with my laughter and burned holes into batik table cloths with the acid that fell from my eyes. I am Wednesday's child. But I have swallowed a star. And if I live half my lifetime in my last few minutes, I guess that'll be alright.

I create the world by apprehending it. My mind and my sense organs sculpt empty space and vibrant sub-atomic particles into objects and could just as well create them otherwise ... your foot the resonant drumstick on the resonant skin of the pavement, for instance, rather than the argyled extremity of your leg. I have created you by looking at, touching, hearing or making love to you. just as your disordered perceptions have created a beautiful griffin. I went to Madison Avenue after I left the King of Seville, you know. It was during the nineteen sixties and people on one side of the world were rejoicing in life while their exported countrymen on the other side were incinerating babies with jellied gasoline. I had flown to America with my griffin wings and picked at the window of the agency with my eagle beak but came to the Christmas party as a young woman in a miniskirt. I wore a finely fashioned gold slave bracelet from a caravan of old. I joined Copywriters for Peace. Was I truthful? Tell me. I tried to tell the truth. But I knew the lie was a lie.

At the agency there was a young man who feared that his National Guard unit would be called up for active service. I told him not to go. "But then I would be sent to jail," he said. "And if you go to war, you may be killed," I told him.

"But refusing to go would ruin my career." "So would death." But he could not be reasoned with, shook like the ancients who were terrified by my griffin form, made his peace with murdering and being murdered in exchange for the promise of an office with wall-to-wall carpeting and lime-colored curtains.

I fled to the countryside where I planted fields of love and reaped a crop of sorrow. My neighbors, lonesome for modernity, imported noise by the bale. A man was murdered on the farm up the road. The police said that God had ordained it but that it was a clearcut case of free will. Whose free will? Certainly not the victim's. I decided it was time to progress to no progress. Fatalism is not chosen. It is decreed by fate. Wishing to flee deeper into the country I burrowed into the hillside. I emerged in the heart of the city. I rose above the city and found the sky a forest of green.

In that green sky, in that second countryside, at last I grew old. I was always old; the beginning of a thing is the beginning of its end. My beak became blunt, my pains became sharp, the hot flame of my sensuality became a slow simmer. I knew I was old because I was told I was young. To compliment an old griffin by calling her young is like complimenting a black person by calling him white, or a woman by calling her a man. These are the insults imparted by the friendly.

In my great antiquity, I tore with my talons at the pretensions of my being. No matter how old you are, if you acknowledge that your life has been a lie, it becomes the truth. I began emerging from the nightmare of greatness and discovered I have nowhere to go. I immersed myself in the culture I came from, broke with that culture, realised that even the idea of getting free of the culture comes from the culture itself. I pecked with my splintering beak at the keyboard of a word processor. I abandoned revenge. I was one of the dancing geriatrics of the writers' brigade. My friends began dying. Priests spoke irrelevantly of respect for the dead, who no longer needed it. I quit the church. It has no room for griffins anyway.
Organized religion is a contradiction in terms.

I have been a hundred times divorced and a thousand times widowed and now I am alone. It is the misfortune of the female, even the female time-traveling griffin, to outlive her lovers. And yet it is her fortune too, for it gives her time for reflection. I have spent entire evenings wondering where the me's were that I'd left at various turnings in the road but have largely abandoned memory in favor of abstract thought since reflection is existence, and better than to remember is to be. I have reflected on men inventing women and on women inventing men and griffins, and on the indivisibility of love. Opening my senses to smell in my wild untended garden, I have learned that the soul is the navigator of the mind. Trapped in the gorse, I have learned to cry for help. Licking my wounds, I have unleashed the healing power of my own saliva, known to every beast, forgotten by man who unlearns what nature knows and then rediscovers it from a book. Flying wearily along the highway of night, I have seen inert argon's theft of colors. I have surrendered myself to the creative force of madness and the sometime wisdom of fate. I have screamed in my sleep about the murder of language. I have broken chains of water. Mused about the irrelevancy of both theory and pragmatism. Chuckled at the Allah Akbar tautology.

You may think it odd for a griffin to keep a radio in her nest. But I do. My wings are tired and molt so often and I don't get around much anymore. I was listening to a science program one day. Someone had devised a method of confirming that falls from high places were likely to shorten a person's life.

An experimental group of five hundred people were pushed from the top of the Empire State Building. A control group, also of five hundred, were not. There were significantly more fatalities in the experimental group. This is science. I've lived. I've loved. I've traveled. I've remembered. I've reflected. Having done all this, I'm none the wiser. Having discovered this, I'm wiser.

FROM THE MEMOIRS OF A ZEN BUTTERFLY

I have a confession to make. I dreamed you were still living here and you were working at the university on a cycle of nine days on and one day off so that, of course, the day of the week that you had off kept shifting. You got to choose your first day off though and you chose the Sunday, even though you had only worked three days by then. You told me you did that because that way people would be less aware of what you did on your day off and that you resented the scrutiny because you felt that that way they'd know if you fell in love with someone. I resented that because I wanted an exclusive on your love. I guess that's the most painful dream I've ever had to admit to, seeing as I'm trying so hard to be a Buddha or a Butterfly or at the very least someone committed to Total Truth, Metatruth and eventually even Excursions Beyond Metatruth, and here this dream shows me as a jealous Son of a Butterfly like everyone else. I want to take the world with me to a brighter place and enter the world's darkness to understand, and the world takes _me_ with _it_. It's all so goddamn tricky.

Aristotle said the truth was in the middle. In the middle of what? One person says there's no god and another says there are many. Does that mean there's some?

They were debating just the other day at the Greek Academy. They were trying to figure out what is Man. Leaving aside the implicit sexism, ageism, et cetera and remembering that this _is_, after all, Ancient Greece, let's eavesdrop on them as well as _look_ what's going on.

One of the scholars decides, "Man is a featherless biped." As they'd been working their asses to the bone pondering the various possibilities while the lucky slaves got on with cooking and chopping wood and easier shit like that, the Smart People decided to call it a night, have a few beers or whatever it is they drank in Ancient Greece. (I doubt that ouzo had been invented yet.) And then sleep on it. When they got up in the morning to resume their deliberations, they found a plucked chicken on the table. They voted five to four that it was not a man. (Democracy started in Greece, you know, even if slaves, women, children, et cetera were excluded.)

"Well," said Aristotle. (Actually, that's not what he said because he was speaking Ancient Greek although he didn't know it was Ancient. (He thought it was Modern.) But I've translated this into English because pretty much aside from the alphabet which renegade mathematicians do tend to retain, I don't know the original Greek, which makes me a very suitable translator.) "let's" (remember this is still sort of Aristotle speaking) "say Man is a Rational Animal."

"Was whoever plucked that chicken rational?" someone else asks.

They met for weeks and weeks until someone said they had a deadline to meet because the world was about to end and it would be very untidy if they hadn't first decided what the hell Man was. They had called a public hearing on the matter and one thousand (approximately) free (approximately) men (?) were presenting white papyruses, green papyruses, consultation papyruses und so weiter (ha!) and they were nowheres near a settlement, with opinion divided pretty much down the middle as to whether Man was a rational animal or a featherless biped.

One minute before the end of the last hour, an emergency compromise was finally reached. Man, it was decided, was a semirational slightly feathered monoped.

God was so busy laughing that he forgot to destroy the world.

Anyway, truth being in the middle, I really should call this "Confessions of a Slightly Feathered Semirational Monoped." But that would be less elegant than "Memoirs of a Zen Butterfly."

Even less elegant than admitting how much I love you.

EXCURSION BEYOND METATRUTH

What lies below the molten rock? What cool blue configurations exist in the scarlet fire? Can I describe to myself in words that would have meaning to one who has never seen? Why should I photograph the exhilarating sky of first light or the dismal pale grey of arctic noon or the star-pierced blackness of night? Why should I learn piano, guitar, molecular biology, business administration, trade union history or methods of replication of the various keys that already exist to my already open self? The chiropodist must not take a chisel to me for I too have feet of clay. Why do I love the elegant ghost who in sprung meter anticipated eternity after death when it already enveloped her in life, permeated her being, wove through butterflies and bees and flowers and yes unerupted volcanoes and earthquakes beyond happening because it is the very fibre of everything we are made of? It is the time of the Grand Inquisition. There is a confessional box and on both sides of it a mirror. The mirrors are empty, reflecting each other, confessing to each other ... their fullness. The television is on ... rare in the days of the G. I., and we see two psychoanalysts back to back furiously scribbling on their note pads.

There is no patient ... their fees are too exorbitant to make one possible. I return from the world of imagination and look out of my window at blue clouds drifting slowly across an almost pink sky. What is imagination? Image-ination. I express in images the feelings that images impress on me. I howl with a sorrow bordering on elation. It is not raining outside but it is pouring in my soul. Our collective soul that stretches beyond our petty concerns, myopias and yours to what a blind person can see with clarity, to what the deaf can hear, to the hungry mouth of the unbounded universe beyond time, space and tigers burning bright illuminating night, casting cosmic shadows over day, the drifting clouds now edged with pale intimations of softly rebellious apricots ... beyond saying, beyond telling. Und wenn d'rebbe tenzt ...

the rabbi dances ... the mountain quakes!

OUTSIDE TIME

> "the mind is its own beautiful prisoner"
> - e.e. cummings

Make no mistake about it. I sometimes enjoy my exile. It is in some sense a return. As I was telling you, I began as some sort of separate entity when my father's seed which hadn't even had time to properly compose itself, defensive in its disorientation, penetrated my mother's egg already extant when she began, when these dissimilar elements just had to learn to co-exist in some way or other with that transcendental self that we already were, that self that had been illuminated by torch-bearers as diverse as Thoreau, Baldwin, Kahlo, people like that and nevertheless cast dark shadows that with my persistent gaze, I never really saw in this my personal time.

One of the many turning points of my life and of yours as well, one of those moments in our time like that when Whitman, in a once, walked out of an observatory and looked up and wrote, was when Camus died. I never read Camus ... It helps if you're revering someone, if you've never read them.

My evening session lit prof brought out a mag that interviewed Camus. Following that, Camus went home to France, if existentialists have homes and one foggy night wrapped his car around a tree the way philosophers among others, often do. Word got to Condé Nast and they bought republication rights and published it in one of their mags – Cosmopolitan I think. A patina of wisdom accordingly accrued to all touched by this and tens upon tens of thousands of catastrophes.

About a decade later the numbers went haywire. Bitter battles went on about the right way to make sense of things like mayonnaise statistics and talking airplanes.

My boss at the ad agency was fired. The bosses no longer wanted his wisdom. Eventually he got a better job.

The guy they brought in over me was jealous of his fiefdom. I was informed that if I wanted to stay on I would have to relinquish my nights to the pursuit of a Ph D in business statistics ... Not my cup of poetry.

Remember this was still the sixties just. Some guy I gave a flower to on my lunch hour needed a tenth for a minyan. The little synagogue was one flight up. Later, coming out of the shul, I saw the gypsy tea room next door. I went in for a reading. The prognosticator who came with the tea cup told me that within a month (!) I would successfully complete the project I needed to finish. Notwithstanding the numerous fissures in the statistical community it was self evident that lady didn't know her ass from a tea leaf. This was my life work she was talkin about. My karma. Ydon't make light of shit like that.

This pen is my scalpel. It cuts open my soul. In my soul I hope to find all of humanity and more. If this be a vain hope it beats a lot of things that were going on. Some poor nut case trepanated himself with a power drill. Years before I'd known someone who knew someone who had electric shock. There are two kinds of lunatic in the world. Those who are crazy and know it. And those who don't know it. My father was of the latter kind. Some of the latter kind become scoutmasters. If you've got a father like that you've got to go crazy. Otherwise the world wouldn't make any sense at all.

Merit badges did not save my soul.

Nostradamus was lucky. He lived in an era before merit badges. He had to be lucky because he was sad. His first wife and the children they had together had died. And it was after that that he learned about boiling things three times to make sure they were sterile. Maybe this was in case you forgot the other two times or maybe as a nod in the direction of trinity. Anyhow no-one was boiling anything then and this was long before Pasteur but long after the Book of Job which Nostradamus will have doubtless read in the original Hebrew. He fell in love again and he and his second wife had children together. Word got out that Nostradamus could tell the future. He couldn't even tell the past. But he was some sort of proto-existentialist. So he was drafted which is to say Catherine di-Medici sent for him. Ordered him to leave the wife and kids at home and tell fortunes at her court. At court he learned that Catherine di-Medici intended to have any Huguenots remaining on the continent of Europe executed on Valentine's Day. He sent word to them secretly and they split for places like Cornwall and Wales. I don't like Valentine's Day. First Valentine's Day in my life there was a massacre. Al Capone had a crush on a prima donna at the Chicago Opera, who had a voice that could melt volcanos. He always brought her flowers. But in 1929 about eight months before the crash he missed a performance. On Valentine's day he was in Florida. The rest of his mob was in police uniforms in Chicago shooting people on suspicion of being alive. I don't know where my elementary school graduation book is. All the girls wrote in it cuz I had the cutest stutter. Roses are red. Violets are blue.

The steamer trunks were already packed when my second wife introduced me to Phoebe from Condé Nast who volunteered to do a Tarot. That was the first Tarot I ever had. Also the last. I don't believe Phoebe was a method actress. I believe that she believed in what she was doing and that she did it with integrity. Also she was smart. A lot smarter than the woman in the tea room. And she seemed to understand what I was reaching for. I didn't want to prejudice the reading by telling her too much – that I was working on a book that had changed its name several times – a collection of poems. Or a novel that I later abandoned. Anyhow, Phoebe, normally a cheerful type, went pale. She said she saw exile, imprisonment and death. She was so convincing that I never told anyone until today. This was not like other forms of divination that lent themselves to enough interpretations to keep you coming back for more until you finally outgrow them as well. So I lived much of the rest of my life – maybe in some sense all of it – under the shadow of Phoebe's prophesy.

You know that time at the Abbey maybe ten or twenty years ago when different people were doing different things to help raise money for the Abbey. There was a kind guy who was doing Tarots for a nominal fee. I wouldn't have considered approaching him for a reading. It would have been like challenging the gods, whether or not the gods existed. In that sense I was already in prison, in a prison made of words. The events in the world at large were pretty much as crazy as they'd always been. I was bound to see my universe through the prism of self-fulfilling prophesy.

I've always been suggestible. I could think of hundreds of examples. Lull the listener or the reader into the ubiquitous trance that is my time. None of us has time for that luxury anymore but it is necessary to sketch some of the highlights, not to dust all my impressions under the throwrug of dreaming. I left my country one month later than I intended and one month after that in Ohio all hell broke loose. Roses were no longer red.

It is hard to say who was more powerful – Doctor Osner or Mr Armitage. Mr Armitage was one of my high school lit teachers. In his opinion my stutter wasn't cute. This was after all an all boys science high school. The heart of what we were meant to get to, the heart of it was the heart of time. His lit class was only in composition so for his time he referred me to Doctor Osner. She was originally from Vienna, an Adlerian analyst, with offices uptown, up the street from the Half

Moon Hotel. There was powerful symbolism in that alone. The Half Moon had been the name of Henry Hudson's ship.

He had traded some glass beads for the whole island of Manhattan. At a later time Janet Frame wrote that she had traded her safety for the glass beads of fantasy. I'm not sure who got the bargain in all of this. I know that I agree with Vasily Grossman that what matters – the real revolution – is kindness. Or as a song-writer in Berlin was to observe in 1969, the revolution to be a revolution must cast the first stone at itself.

It was not courtesy of Doctor Osner that I eventually got rid of most of my stutter. She sat in a dark room behind an enormous desk and the me she explained to me was not me. The me I was looking for was everyone. The me I was looking for was you.

Like everyone, especially every ageing person, I don't remember everything but things come back from long long ago, like being tied in my crib at night so I wouldn't disturb my young parents, regarding it a challenge and slipping out, Houdini-style only to become a disciplinarian myself as a young adult when my son broke the bars of his playpen with its multicolored abacus-like beads. You know the other night when I spoke to you on the phone after coming out of a deep sleep and for the moment I couldn't remember what $\frac{1}{2}+\frac{1}{4}$ was or find the words to say so. That was like hypnotic regression ... like when Doctor Barnley in New Jersey counted me down into the past and asked me what I saw there and what I heard. I had started elementary school. The teacher - if you could call her that – for the first two years was Miss Waugh, only I thought it was spelled War. She humiliated all us boys by watching us all lined up at a row of urinals gushing tragically. But this was one of those rare Saturdays off and I was walking with my father. I said "I want my mommy" and broke away from him, turning to the right on Coney

Island Avenue to find my mother at the candy shop she worked at. It took him blocks to overtake me and then instead of explaining that the shop lay in the opposite direction, he beat the living shit out of me.

I didn't know that much about my maternal grandparents' musical tastes. I knew they liked Rachmaninoff. It is said that the third piano concerto is his most autobiographical. It concludes with a crescendo. It's back to begin again. It's impossible to include everything. There are too many acts waiting to go on stage ... look at this pile of notes lying next to me. Suffice it to say, my mother found love several times after my father died. I and my descendants – my whole world owe their existence to so many things. One of them is that under the pressures of her day she hitched up with the wrong guy. I'm selfish enough to be glad that she did. And to hope that everyone I've loved, however imperfectly, is glad of that too.

Most of the schisms that occur are within ourselves. This is not to say that we're to blame. Nor that we're blameless. It's just a statement of fact.

In the end I got some of my talents from my father, from my antecedents, from everyone I've ever loved and from their antecedents. Listen – Phoebe – exile ain't half bad. Even if imagination were all there was – Wow.

Anyhow, this story is to the memory of my mother, who was born a hundred years ago this year.

And here I am. Deep in inner space. Outside time.

"Do I contradict myself?
Very well then I contradict myself,
(I am large, I contain multitudes.)"
- Walt Whitman
(Song of Myself)

"All waves run shorewards
But there is no centre to the ocean
Where they all arise."
- Rebecca Elson
(A Responsibility to Awe)

"That happiness endures which comes
from the grinding together of
anguish and ecstasy, and from the
intensity of the grinding."
- Hung Tzu-ch'eng
(Discourses on Vegetable Roots)